CRACKING THE CODE TO MARITAL BLISS

How to go from Pain, Frustration and Boredom to Passion, Pleasure and Purpose

JAMES T. HORNING
with
KIMBERLY A. HORNING

ISBN: 978-1986123334

One Woman Man Media, LLC.

WARNING!

This book is not for everybody. It's for the 5% that refuse to accept less than a passionate, blissful or even a truly transcendent experience. That's not to say you won't benefit from it if you have lower expectations for yourself. If you have a hungry mind and a yearning heart, you will receive as much as you can hold. I say this because if you adopt the paradigm I have for you, it's possible to have a mind-altering relationship with your lover (mate). By "mind-altering" I mean an experience that far exceeds what most have ever witnessed or believed possible—one that changes your perception of everything, evolves your personal psychology, and transcends the earthly, giving you a glimpse of the divine.

There are those that have labeled (even criticized) this work as being "way out there", not mainstream enough, and even esoteric. They don't think that people are ready for it, that we're all just too self-centered and hedonistic to embrace and embody such a profound message. I want to believe they're wrong. I think people are moving to a higher level of consciousness that's starving for change, hungry for a higher standard to live by, and thirsting for inspiration.

DISCLOSURE & DISCLAIMER

If your marriage or relationship is in a crisis situation, please seek the help of a qualified professional counselor or schedule a private weekend with us. If you both want to save your marriage and are willing to do whatever it takes, send us an email at info@greatmarriagegreatlife.com. On a very limited basis, we offer private interventions with guaranteed results.

I could be wrong about everything, just so you know. Knowledge is fluid and with very few absolutes. However, adopting and embracing the concepts in this book will more than likely transform your marriage and your life. That said, they may not change anything for you. It all depends on you, your willingness to grow, and your level of consciousness. A good marriage may be formulaic but a great marriage is divinely inspired by your highest self.

You will notice that this book seems as if it is written mostly by my hand. That's because it is. I've included my wife, Kimberly, as a co-author because for all practical purposes, she is. My marriage to her has been the initial litmus test for all the ideas, concepts and philosophies presented herein. Her willingness to challenge my ideas and respond authentically to my approaches have been a valuable proving ground, as have been the countless dynamic conversations we've had over the years and still have almost daily. She provides the yin to my yang, the Venus to my Mars, and the softness to my edge. Without her, this book would not exist. You will find her comments and insights sprinkled throughout the book like sparkling opals on a beach of sand, and appropriately noted by butterflies, which she embodies in human form.

In the spirit of full disclosure, a small portion of the content is borrowed verbatim from my first book *Winning at the Game of Wife*.

**Marriage is art. Art is life.
Life is discovering our divinity.**
—In homage to the incomparable Spar Street.

CONTENTS

ACKNOWLEDGMENTS

First and foremost, I want to thank my wife Kimberly for her amazing love, enduring patience and divine inspiration. My commitment to being the husband she deserves has compelled me, driven me and inspired me to go way, way, way beyond my own imagined limits of personal growth and development. Without her, this book certainly would not exist.

I want to recognize a few others who have been positively influential in the shaping of my life including my mom Kathy, my grandfather Dr. Merritt Horning, and my uncle Phil Horning.

I also want to recognize a few giants who I greatly esteem for their contributions to the fields of marriage, inspiration and personal development, and on whose shoulders I stand. In no particular order, these remarkable people are Tony Robbins, Dr. David Schnarch, Dr. John Gray, Dr. Willard F. Harley Jr., Esther Perel, Mihaly Csikszentmihalyi, Wayne Dyer, Richard Bach, Napoleon Hill, Deepak Chopra and Zig Ziglar.

WHO ARE THESE PEOPLE AND WHY SHOULD YOU LISTEN TO THEM?

Hi there, my name is James T. Horning. My friends call me Tad. I am a husband, father, lover, strategic marriage coach, mountain biker, relationship philosopher, Tuscan cook, horse wrangler, wood worker and wine enthusiast, in that order.

My wife, Kimberly, and I are the creators of the www.GreatMarriageGreatLife.com couples training programs that include online training, private coaching and live events. We are really, really passionate about marriage. In fact, we think being married is the greatest thing since chocolate and peanut butter. I can boast that I've been happily married to the same woman for 29 years and counting. That's not to say that my marriage to Kimberly has been a perpetual fairy tale. It's more a marvelous adventure that might be likened to backpacking across Europe or sailing around the world. It would be an understatement to say that it has been the most challenging part of my life right up to the point when we had a baby girl (at which point I was met with new challenges I never dreamed of). It's also been the juiciest and most fulfilling part of my life and it just keeps getting better. Sharing your life with someone who consistently challenges you, baffles you, and often drives you out of your friggin' mind, is the greatest gift you can experience once you grasp the grand scheme behind it all. So stay with me, you won't be disappointed.

I began my life as a marriage trainer and influencer about 9 years ago, right about the time my wife and I celebrated our 20th wedding anniversary. I surprised Kimberly with a Hawaiian-style vow renewal ceremony on a beach in Maui. Our vows didn't so much need renewing as much as I just wanted to show her how enthusiastic I was about spending the rest of my life with her. What a rock star move that was, right?

Well, as our celebration progressed and the joy and hilarity of the event built to a crescendo, it became evident to our guests that we weren't just token newlyweds but that we had never really ever stopped acting like newlyweds. What was the *secret* they asked? What are you doing, after 25 years together, that makes you seem so genuinely in love and passionate for each other? Those are the questions I will answer for you in this book. But first, I need to finish the story.

As the tropical libations began to have their effect, my normal shyness seemed to fade with the Maui sunset. So, I willingly and with great pleasure answered these most profound questions about love and marriage. Our distinguished guests must have either been very impressed or very patronizing because at least 2 suggested I write a book on the subject. Well, that being the fourth or fifth time someone had suggested this to me, I felt it was about time to heed the calling and get started.

Not being one to do anything half-assed, I decided to corroborate my ideas and philosophies with what was being taught by the leading experts in the field. After my personal wake-up call that you'll learn about in the next chapter, I had started reading and improving my skills as a husband, but now I had a renewed fervor. So, I started reading and reading and reading. Kimberly and I collaboratively read over 100 books on marriage, relationship psychology, and sexuality; attended numerous relationship seminars and certification programs, looking for the magic potion, the universal blueprint, the secret sauce. I wanted to understand better what I was doing right and formulate it in a way that I could communicate to others. Along the way, we discovered that many (maybe most) of the "experts" in the marriage and relationship space weren't that expert at all. They had the traditional credentials everyone is accustomed to seeing after their names but they weren't "life experience" qualified to teach you how to have an enduring passionate marriage. In other words, they had clinical knowledge but no experiential knowledge. Worse than that, they were (are) often total hypocrites already on their second or third marriages. That's when we decided we didn't want to be victims of what we *didn't* know about having a great marriage. That set us on the quest to go deeper than we ever imagined we would.

Out of that was born my first book *Winning at the Game of Wife: How to make your woman love you, want you and adore you like never before* (Morgan

James Publishing). It was written for men in a language that I thought would resonate with a guy's guy, if you know what I mean. Little did I know that my biggest audience and fan base would be women. After all, what woman wouldn't love a book that teaches men how to get what they want by being the man that their wife deserves. In fact, one reader shared with me that the dynamic in his relationship was improving simply by virtue of the fact that his wife *knew* he was reading the book and he hadn't even done anything different!

Well, fast forward a few years. Kimberly and I have taken our relationship to an even higher level and are really excited to share the distinctions we've made. We've realized that a "good" marriage isn't the goal anymore; that "good" is actually a low standard. We've discovered deeper levels of connection that can only be experienced with time, commitment, personal growth, and a strong desire to love each other the way that we each deserve. It has really been like seeing the code behind The Matrix. We've uncovered that certain *je ne sais quoi*, that elusive missing ingredient, that when added to the mix seems to miraculously change everything in the twinkling of an eye.

Your *je ne sais quoi* is in here and only you will know what it is when you find it. It will be that idea, concept or practice that instantly fills a void, completes a picture, or gives you a life-changing epiphany. If you're anything like me, you'll probably experience a series of "aha moments" and paradigm shifts that will collectively change how you see and do your relationship forever.

WHY THE GODS ARE LAUGHING

The year was about 4,000 BC give or take, or about 6,000 years ago. An extraordinary and historical event happened. According to one of the greatest literary works of all time, a celestial cause was set in motion; an institution was ordained; a gift was given.

God gave Adam a wife. No doubt her beauty was beyond compare. In fact, it had no comparison. I think it's safe to presume that she was perfect in every way and that her mental capacity, i.e., intelligence, reasoning, judgment, insightfulness, intuition and cleverness, was at an all-time high.

Now Adam, presumably the epitome of a man, must have been a pillar of physical strength and magnificence. After all he was created in God's image. His mental capacity may have even been equal to God's except for one thing: he lacked an experiential knowledge of good and evil.

But not to worry, the woman that God has given him will soon help to enlighten him before he even has a chance to give her a name.

Now chronologically speaking, God makes a woman for Adam in Genesis 2:22; one sentence later in Genesis 2:23 Adam says, "I'm going to call her "woman" because she was taken out of me"; one sentence later in Genesis 2:24 it suggests that "they shall become one flesh"; immediately followed in Genesis 2:25 by "and they were naked and not ashamed".

In 10 short sentences, the Bible tells part of an epic story that goes like this: God says "man should not be alone" so God makes woman; God says that they should become one flesh; they are both naked and not ashamed. What do you think would naturally happen next in this sequence?

Now I'm assuming that your imagination has conjured up some visual images of what is happening here. In case it hasn't, I'll share mine with you.

They are in the Garden of Eden. It's paradise. The sky is azure blue; it's 72 degrees with a soft breeze; rivers and streams flowing with wine, milk and honey flow through the forever green meadows of perfectly manicured grass that never needs mowing. Trees and vines bearing luscious mangoes, guavas, grapes and forbidden fruit are in abundance.

Eve is gloriously naked and magnetizing; a nectar-bearing orchid, a ripe, juicy peach. Adam is naked and his towering magnificence sends an unfamiliar quiver down Eve's spine. And not insignificantly, they are not ashamed. Adam is quite taken with Eve's inner goodness and heavenly beauty. Her feminine essence is polarizing to him. In fact, he is quite compelled to fulfill that "shall become one flesh" prophecy stated just 4 sentences back in his life.

So he says "Hey Eve darling, what do you say we, uh, you know, become one flesh?" Well, being a woman, Eve unwittingly throws Adam his first curve ball and says "That's sounds really nice, Honey, but I'm hungry. Why don't we go find something to eat first? Then we can come back and find a nice soft place in the grass over by that stream flowing with White Zinfandel. And after we've had a couple glasses of wine and talked a bit, I'll take you on a trip to heaven and back that you'll never forget."

The next thing you know, their wedding night is epically messed up. They meet a serpent, Eve eats some forbidden fruit, she offers it to Adam, and because he's thinking with his penis and can't think about anything other than visiting Eve's secret garden, like an idiot, he eats some. The next thing they know, whoosh-bang-zap, they're wearing fig leaves and getting kicked out of paradise.

Now you may think you know the rest of the story, but do you?

This is the first recorded, at least the most well-known beginning of the most perplexing arrangement ever conceived. Yes, I am talking about marriage.

What was presumably invented by God, ordained in heaven, and followed as a cultural practice by most people on earth past and present, is either one of the most ludicrous, ridiculous and absurd arrangements ever plotted or possibly the most brilliant scheme ever conceived.

Is the marriage of a man and woman the perfect cosmic joke or is it a divine gift given to us by God herself? That question I will heroically attempt to answer in the following pages.

Some believe that marriages are set up for failure from the beginning. Men and women are too different—oil and vinegar. We're Mars and Venus after all. We communicate so differently, see things so differently. We seem to have vastly different and often opposing needs.

Why is it that things so often start off with such magic and then eventually go so wrong?

How does animal attraction and romance transition to frustration and disappointment?

How do you go from being in love to getting a divorce?

"For most of us, marriage is like having a Ferrari in our garage that we treat like a pick-up truck. We just don't know what we've got, how to use it or what its grand purpose really is."

Well maybe, just maybe, it's because we don't have a clue what we've got!

For most of us, marriage is like having a Ferrari in our garage that we treat like a pick-up truck. We just don't know what we've got, how to use it or what its grand purpose really is.

I certainly didn't know what I had when I got married. Twelve or thirteen years into my marriage I had a wake-up call that changed my marriage and my life forever!

Kimberly and I were engaged in a heated discussion about something that I'm sure was of no consequence. I don't remember what it was about but I can be certain of 2 things: I was right and she was wrong! In fact, I was usually right and she was usually wrong (I hope you can see the tongue-in-cheek here). And when she didn't acknowledge my logical, objective, all-knowing rightness, it made me crazy. It drove me out of my mind. So I would argue a point until she finally gave in just to make peace. Needless to say, this kind of behavior on my part did not support my lady's attraction to me. In fact, it was the formula for a loss of connection and downright cold bed.

Well, on this day I went too far. As we are speeding up a windy mountain road at about 50 miles per hour, Kimberly became so repulsed by me that she screamed for me to pull the car over so she could relieve herself of my presence. I apparently didn't slow down fast enough because she threw the door open and moved to jump from the car before it stopped. I simultaneously reached over to grab her while skidding to a halt on the side of the road. She immediately jumped out of the car into a cloud of dust and started running back down the road in the direction that we had come from. Thoughts were streaming through my head like "I can't believe this is happening"; "Now I really messed up!"; "This is really embarrassing"; and "How can I make this look like a couple of tourists looking at the view?"

Needless to say, I chased her down the road and coaxed her back to the car. I'm sure the process included a lot of apologies, groveling and eating of crow. I think I actually developed a taste for crow.

In the days and weeks that followed, I did a lot of thinking and soul searching. In reflecting back on the incident and many other similar incidents, I was confronted with my shortcomings as a husband and as a human being. I realized that I was not being the husband that my wife deserved. I realized that my narcissistic need to *be right* was causing her a lot of pain and that my requirement to *make sense* out of her emotional needs created a chasm between us. I began to see that I had beliefs and rules about love and marriage that were sabotaging the full potential of our relationship and that I had been consistently hurting the most significant person in my life. I realized that I needed to grow or risk losing the person I loved most.

So, I dug deep and did what any other guy in my position would do, I went on a month-long hunting/fishing/golfing trip to Canada. No, not really! What I did do though, was consciously choose to be more of the man that my wife deserved. I decided to choose her over my ego-driven need to be right, and make sense of her feminine attributes, and stop trying to change her. I learned to embrace and honor our differences at a new level. And then something extraordinary happened! I saw our marriage like I had never seen it before. I felt like I got a sneak peek behind the wizard's curtain.

Years later I would be inspired with a strong desire to corroborate my new vision of marriage with the "experts" in the field. But it wasn't until I looked at everything that I had learned through the lens of my own marriage and love affair with my wife that it hit me. It was like seeing the digital coding behind the Matrix for the first time.

I saw it with crystal clarity. Marriage is the elixir of life! It is Life's Holy Grail.

Where else can you get love, sex, passion, excitement, significance, certainty, variety, meaning, purpose, challenge, personal growth and spiritual experience all in one place? It's the ultimate classroom, playground and sanctuary all rolled into one! There is no other environment that requires, inspires and compels you to grow as a human being in virtually every facet.

"Marriage is the elixir of life! It is Life's Holy Grail."

Marriage is life's grandest pursuit and like any grand pursuit it will push you to your absolute limits—that is, if you're doing it right.

But isn't that the way it is with any pursuit worthy of your effort? When we want to be good at something and experience it at a high level, what do we do? We learn everything we can about it. We take classes, courses and lessons. We hire coaches and trainers. We find mentors. We hang out with people who have a higher level of mastery than we do. We find inspiring examples to emulate.

"Marriage is life's grandest pursuit and like any grand pursuit it will push you to your absolute limits— that is, if you're doing it right."

Is the pursuit of mastery of anything ever easy? It never is! Is it worth it? Immensely!

Personally, I've learned that my relationship is not only my biggest opportunity for personal growth and rewarding challenge in life, but it's also my biggest source of enjoyment, fulfillment and meaning. And amazingly, through my marriage I have the power to influence my children, my family, my friends and my community. Through my marriage I have the influence to make the world a better place.

Our marriages are the platform for major shifts in societal values and trends because we are generally responsible for where the next generation get their values, their examples of relationships, and models for how to live their life.

"Through my marriage I have the influence to make the world a better place."

Our children learn love and humility from us; also things like commitment, perseverance and communication.

They learn about morality, ethics and integrity.

They learn about romance, sexuality and desire.

Through our relationships, they learn about God, or not!

But somewhere in the chaos of life, we get distracted and lose sight of what really matters. Maybe we never really thought about it. Somehow the mundane, the trivial, and often the ridiculous become the focus of our attention.

When it comes to our mates and our relationships, we often take our eye off the ball. We get frustrated, resentful and discontent because we are focusing on the grime on the chrome wheels, the parking lot dings on the doors and the minor cracks in the leather seats completely forgetting that what we really have is a gorgeous red Ferrari—and that if we love it, take care of it, and show it some gratitude, it will put a big stupid grin on our face.

Somewhere we lose sight of the idea that our mate was given to us as a divine gift. Or maybe we never really knew! They represent those attributes of God that only the opposite sex can reveal. Without them, we have an incomplete picture of everything that is and ever will be.

> *"Somewhere we lose sight of the idea that our mate was given to us as a divine gift. Or maybe we never really knew! They represent those attributes of God that only the opposite sex can reveal. Without them, we have an incomplete picture of everything that is and ever will be."*

The problems that seem to arise as a result of our inherent differences actually aren't problems at all. They are merely signals for us to fully realize our potential as human beings and make a meaningful difference in the world.

Incidentally, these "grow signals" are available only within the context of intimate relationships. Your relationships with friends, colleagues and coworkers can never provide the leverage you need to make real and lasting changes in your psychology, your behaviors, or your beliefs.

And when we give up on our marriages too soon, we short-change ourselves of the opportunity to accelerate our personal development as a human being and contributor to humanity.

To help you get your head in the right place, answer these questions. After you read each question, close your eyes as you answer it in your head.

> *"And when we give up on our marriages too soon, we short-change ourselves of the opportunity to accelerate our personal development as a human being and contributor to humanity."*

What would happen if I consciously honored my wedding vows?

What would happen if I started honoring my mate for who they are, instead of who I think they should be?

What would happen if I focus on what I love about them and defocus on what bugs me?

What would happen if first thing every morning I expressed my gratitude for *insert mate's name here*?

How differently would I treat them? How would that influence my actions? My communication? My presence with them?

How differently would I feel if I knew that they were entrusted to me for safe keeping?

What might change if I supported my mate's daily needs unselfishly?

What would happen if I helped them pursue their dreams and aspirations? How might that shift the dynamic between us?

What would happen if I reacted to my mate's upsets and blow-ups with patience, kindness and unconditional love?

What would happen if I consistently forgave and forgot as we are admonished to do by most every religious faith in the world?

How would my mate respond to me if I loved them without limit, not expecting anything in return?

How would my marriage change if I renewed daily my choice of mate by consciously pursuing them as if they are a prize worth having?

What would happen if daily, I consciously renewed my vows to love and be faithful with the realization that they are not only my partner in life but also my partner in getting ready for the next?

My friends, the process of being the man or woman that your mate deserves is the journey to the kingdom.

If it isn't the path to godliness it certainly parallels it.

"My friends, the process of being the man or woman that your mate deserves is the journey to the kingdom."

Is the marriage of a man and woman the perfect cosmic joke or is it a divine gift given to us by God? I'll let you be the judge. Just save your judgment for the end of the book. If your heart tells you that it is the latter, then keep reading. If you think that being happy with the opposite sex is limited to uncommitted relationships and casual sex, well just keeping reading anyway so that I have a chance at convincing you otherwise.

WHAT THIS BOOK IS AND ISN'T ABOUT

What this book is about

This book is NOT about how to have a good marriage. It's about how to have a life-long, *passionate,* and blissful marriage. A good marriage happens when you create a safe, certain and predictable environment for each other. The problem with good marriages is that they are "good" right up to the point when they aren't. That is the day when one or both of you tire of the predictability and inherent monotony that comes with too much certainty; or the day when those buried facets of your authentic self that you've been denying to make your marriage "work", suddenly surface and cry for release; or when one of you tires of not having your needs met for things like attention, excitement, adventure, passion or sexual variety.

Contrary to popular belief, "good" actually implies a deficiency. When compared to excellent or outstanding, "good" is obviously missing something; and that something is what this book is all about. It's about resolving the paradox between love and desire, between certainty and uncertainty, and safety and excitement.

By now you've probably realized this isn't just another marriage book. In fact, it's more like the beginning of a crusade or maybe even a vendetta. I know that's strong language and it might even be confusing but the fact of the matter is, I'm really alarmed! I'm disturbed, troubled, distressed and frankly a little ticked off!

Marriages are falling apart all around us and those couples that do stay together rarely

> *"The problem with good marriages is that they are "good" right up to the point when they aren't."*

experience the true potential of their relationship. They might love each other but are starved of the passion, desire and attraction that brought them together in the beginning. They stay together for convenience, fear of change, economic security or out of religious conviction or habitual mediocrity. They unwittingly settle for a marginal experience that is but a poor quality facsimile of the real thing.

As you can guess, I'm all for preserving the institution of marriage. It is now my life's work. But my definition of preservation is different than most. Most people and even most experts have taken a Procrustean approach to defining marriage and what one's expectations should be.

In Greek mythology, Procrustes was the owner of an estate situated along the road between the cities of Athens and Eleusis. Procrustes was a most hospitable host (some versions say he was an abductor) to weary travelers; inviting them to stay for dinner and a bed. He is most notably remembered by his penchant for ensuring that his beds fit his guests perfectly. But rather than modify the beds to fit the guests, he modified the guests to fit his beds. How he did this I'll leave to your imagination and spare you the gory details.

The Procrustean bed is a metaphor for how often, when faced with limited knowledge, understanding and insight, we resolve a philosophical quandary by manufacturing models or paradigms that fit with what we believe to be true or want to be true, rather than questioning and expanding our own thinking.

How does this relate to marriage? In 2 ways. First, as I suggested earlier, we have relegated our Ferrari (marriage) to utility pick-up truck status out of sheer naiveté, cultural conditioning and an unwillingness to believe that it isn't marriage as an institution that needs fixing, but rather us as human beings that need cultivating, honing and elevating. The marriage (life-long monogamous commitment) between a man and woman is the perfect environment for the latter and is a repeating theme throughout this book.

The second way the Procrustean bed metaphor relates to marriage is what got me all fired up to write this book. You see, there is a prevailing belief and expectation that "romantic love" does not last and that in a committed relationship it transitions to what is known as "mature love" or "real love". This widely taught and broadly accepted misconception has tainted the minds of the masses, lowered their expectations, lulled them into complacency and generally short-changed them of their true potential.

The idea that a couple in a committed long-term relationship cannot and are not likely to maintain "romantic love", i.e., the desire, attraction and passion of their courtship, is based largely on convention as well as on the research of celebrated anthropologist, Helen Fisher. In her book *Why We Love*, the love that a human experiences in a committed relationship is broken into 3 stages: Lust, Romantic Love and Attachment. The final stage presupposes that Lust and Romantic Love are historical waypoints once Attachment (bonding and commitment) is achieved. In other words, the desire and attraction that is associated with romance is a passing and unsustainable experience. I personally think this theory is a welcome rationale for those who have not been able to sustain desire and passion in their own relationships despite their expertise. They want to believe that it's out of their control! Often, if an "expert" cannot maintain or reproduce romantic love in their own relationship, then it must be a human impossibility; an anomaly at best.

I actually don't fault anyone for this because until now, there has been no other model. It's the best paradigm we've had. After all, the chemicals and hormones that your body produces to get you to fall in love and want to mate with the opposite sex begin to dissipate after 18 months or so of engagement with a particular person. In other words, once nature and instinct have fulfilled their purpose of preventing human extinction, you're left with 2 choices. Either abandon the person you're with in a new search for that lovin' feeling or settle in (emphasis on "settle") for the long haul. Neither of these options are very fulfilling, nor do they acknowledge the magic, divinity or intention of this gift we call marriage.

This is where my ideology about marriage and romantic love diverges from the masses. Most marriage educators are instructing couples on how to have a "good" marriage by teaching them how to communicate, compromise and negotiate to have their needs met. Many "experts" want to "preserve" marriage in a way that might be likened to pumping it full of formaldehyde. Developing a good "working relationship" and not getting a divorce doesn't necessarily mean one is married in my book. Monogamy has no inherent virtue, for that matter, if one wishes they were with someone else.

"Developing a good "working relationship" and not getting a divorce doesn't necessarily mean one is married in my book."

Most long-term marriages that we observe are devoid of life, passion and fulfillment. That's not what marriage is supposed to be, at least not any more. The cat is out of the bag for good. We want more, expect more, feel like we deserve more, and rightly so. So when I say my definition of preserving marriage is different, what I mean is I want to bridge the gap between romantic love and "mature" enduring love, and back again. I want to propose that in marriage, romantic love and mature love are two sides of the same coin.

"I want to propose that in marriage, romantic love and mature love are two sides of the same coin."

I want to preserve, expand and enhance the dream that got you to say "I do" in the beginning. I actually want to grow it to a more inspiring and virtuous place than it has ever been. I want you to see your marriage like you have never seen it before. Does romantic love last in a marriage? The answer is often, rarely. But can it last? ABSOLUTELY! Should it last? Your ability to realize your potential as a human being may depend on it. In fact, it could be the single most rewarding and thrilling pursuit of your life.

So there you have it. That's what this is all about. In this book, you will learn the key ingredients to a deeply loving relationship, a deeply passionate relationship, and a deeply transformational relationship. If you are ready for it, and I think you are, a switch will go off in your brain and you will never see your relationship the same. This is a good thing by the way. If you don't think you can handle it, give the book to someone else.

"Does romantic love last in a marriage? The answer is often, rarely. But can it last? ABSOLUTELY! Should it last? Your ability to realize your potential as a human being may depend on it. In fact, it could be the single most rewarding and thrilling pursuit of your life."

Who this book is for

By virtue of the fact that you have read this far, I can assume that I have your attention and that you are at least intrigued. I believe that you are one of the 3-5% that refuse to settle for mediocrity in your life and are driven to push yourself to new levels. Maybe you're looking for inspiration or hope that there is a magic formula for getting what you want out of your relationship. Either way, I commend and honor you for taking this step towards realizing the true potential of your marriage. We are probably kindred spirits in believing that if something is worth doing, it's worth doing well.

Who this book is NOT for

However, this book may not be for you if you fall in with the majority. Because no matter how you slice it, the 80/20 rule (sometimes it's the 90/10 rule) seems to apply to everything. It's Pareto's principle of distribution and sparsity. Twenty percent of the population make 80% of the money. Eighty percent of a company's revenues come through 20% of their sales people. Eighty percent of our nation's health care costs come from 20% of its population. Twenty percent of professional athletes win 80% of the competitions. And perhaps 20% of the people have 80% of the sex (just guessing on that one). I think you get the idea. This book is written to the 10-20% who want to play full out and make life as rich and juicy as they can. If you want to be the best YOU that you can be; if you want the romance and passion in your marriage to remain alive and even grow more intense over time; if you're ready to play full out, then welcome to our world.

What this book is NOT about

This book is NOT about how to fix your marriage—yet if you even adopt a fraction of the core insights you're about to learn, your marriage will miraculously fix itself.

This book is NOT about how to fix your mate. You can't fix your mate. They probably don't actually need fixing. As you experience a shift in how you see them and how they see themselves, the "fixing" you long for might just sneak itself in there when they're not looking.

This book is NOT about how to fix yourself. You probably don't need fixing either. You are perfect just the way you are. You just need to grow forward in your own divine perfection.

This book is NOT about how to communicate better—however, over time, you will be communicating at a level you've never experienced before.

This book is NOT about how to have more romance. Romance isn't scientific or formulaic. It is a matter of the heart, soul and raw magnetism. Once you've embraced and incorporated the insights I teach into your life and relationship, romance will naturally manifest itself stronger than ever before.

This book is NOT about how to have more sex. More sex, however, is a marvelous bonus feature of applying the principles taught within. To say it is an unintended consequence wouldn't be totally honest.

This book is NOT about how to have better sex. Sike! It's all about how to have the most passionate, mind blowing and deeply profound sex ever! We just don't get into the mechanics and techniques traditionally associated with sex manuals, because the secret to mind-blowing sex is not about positions, techniques or gadgets. It's about desire, personal development, presence, and letting go.

What this book *is* about is How to Turn your Marriage into a Passionate and Meaningful Life-long Love Affair. It is about how to turn your marriage into your LIFE'S ULTIMATE EXPERIENCE. If that inspires you, then join me on this journey.

SETTING THE STAGE

We are not human beings having a spiritual experience. We are spiritual beings having a human experience.

—Pierre Teilhard de Chardin

I've personally come to believe that marriage is the conduit through which we humans may realize our divinity. The divine union between a man and woman, once fully developed, may be the closest exemplification of God that we have. After all, how can one fully understand, comprehend and appreciate what is above without its representation here on earth.

The literature of many prominent spiritual traditions use marriage as a metaphor for the relationship between a god and his/her people. For example, the writings of King Solomon in The Song of Songs are thought by some to be the chronicles of a grand love affair and by others to be a metaphor for God's love for his church. I tend to think it is both. "As it is above, so it is below."

"I've personally come to believe that marriage is the conduit through which we humans may realize our divinity."

"As it is above, so it is below."

What gives a metaphor its power and efficacy is being grounded in human experience, otherwise no one could relate to it. The Song of Songs (aka The Song of Solomon) tells of a passionate relationship that exemplifies love, passion, compassion, patience, kindness, adoration and wonder. These are just a few of the divine qualities that reveal themselves as we nurture a love affair with our mate. The experience of growing as a husband or wife parallels the path of godliness in that it compels and inspires you to realize your highest and best self; that is if you don't resist it.

Spirituality and mastery are kindred in that they are journeys that turn the incomprehensible into the graspable; the complex into the simple; and oftentimes the "something" into nothing. Sometimes, what seems to matter the most in the beginning, doesn't matter at all in the end. This often involves a massive shift in perspective.

"The experience of growing as a husband or wife parallels the path of godliness in that it compels and inspires you to realize your highest and best self."

Mastery at a high level is the taking of something that seems infinitely complex and making it look elegantly simple. Mastery at an even higher level may be "epiphanously" (is that a word?) realizing that the complexity you perceive is not even real at all; that it's a figment of your imagination; that it's a hallucination conjured together by your beliefs, culture, religion, education, family influences, experience and your ego. Because in the end, all the complexities of marriage are but a construct of our ego's need to control and make sense out of our environment. Most of the upsets you have are "rules" and "values" upsets. They happen when we, or our mate, has violated a "rule" that one of us has about something or when we have a values conflict. The crazy thing is that most of our rules and values are nothing but a default program that we adopted from someone else (usually our parents) because it didn't occur to us to do otherwise. In other words, our rules and values often aren't actually really ours to begin with. They aren't necessarily who we really are or who we want to be. And if we think they are us, we often mistakenly try to project them onto our mate who is not us. And in the process, we create unnecessary conflict. In fact, most marital upsets are over things that don't even matter. What does matter is how we handle these upsets and how we use them to grow up as individuals and grow closer as a couple.

Maybe marriage is hard because we've made it hard. Organized religion has historically made salvation hard by manufacturing a complex and painful roadmap that can't be navigated without them. That said, I remember reading a really "good book" once that said "The kingdom of God is within you." Well, I think that in the end, once you've seen beyond Avalon's mists, you'll somehow know that that which you've been working so hard for was already yours all along; and that which you've been seeking for outside yourself has been inside you all along because it's who you are.

"A passionate marriage that rocks your world has infinite complexity. However at some point the complexity transitions to an elegant flow that seems simple on the surface."

This isn't to say that marriage isn't complex.

It's very complex, but in a good way. Much like a great wine is very complex. A passionate marriage that rocks your world has infinite complexity. However at some point the complexity transitions to an elegant flow that seems simple on the surface.

You may think I'm contradicting myself but behind every truth is a paradox. There's a point in every journey towards mastery where you cross over to a place where everything that was hard becomes easy; where the complex appears simple; where the conscious mind gives way to intuition and everything just starts to effortlessly flow. The river is no longer an intricate mass of moving H_2O molecules. It is simply a river. Every accomplished person, whether a pianist, martial artist, musician, athlete, horseman, Wall Street trader or mother has this experience. It's when your heart, brain and spirit seem to sync up and you perform at your best. You're in the timeless present. It's not about you anymore and all the pretense of the temporal world is replaced by an elegant and seamless flow. It just is.

The Japanese word for this experience is "shibumi". Shibumi is one of those words that, like God, to try and describe somehow diminishes and limits it. Nevertheless, a few words and phrases that help to grasp the concept are— *subtle elegance, effortless perfection, elegant simplicity, great refinement underlying common appearance, restrained elegance, and understated excellence.*

To get to this place of flow, or shibumi, is a journey of personal growth and overcoming. It's a process of consistently confronting, recognizing, embracing and meeting the challenges that inevitably come in a relationship and in life for that matter. And then again, it's also a little about just letting go and merging with the river's current instead of trying to swim against it. That said, almost everything in this life that's worth doing usually comes with challenge. The opportunities to enjoy life's richest experiences make us vulnerable to pain, hardship, and suffering. It just goes with the territory. It's how you "use" the opportunities; the perspective that you have on them; and the meaning that you give them that determines the quality of your life. When you see them as they really are—gateways to a higher and richer experience—everything changes.

The problem we most have is that we give up on our relationships too soon. We think because we are having problems that the person we are with is the wrong person and that by finding someone else or changing our circumstances we will solve the problem. In most cases, nothing could be further from the truth. All we end up doing is short-changing ourselves and taking our problems with us to the next relationship.

You see, the problem usually isn't incompatibility or irreconcilable differences. It's usually the lack of understanding what you each need to be doing to meet each other's needs or an unwillingness to do so. And to consistently meet each other's needs at a high level almost always requires personal growth and *spiritual* eyesight. I'd also like to suggest that irreconcilable differences are normal, healthy and even required, to have a deeply meaningful and passionate marriage. What am I talking about? Well, stay with me as we explore that in another chapter.

What comes next?

I'm going to reveal to you what I believe 97% or more of the population doesn't know. Maybe 99%! You're going to learn how to have a passionate marriage that is truly *transcendental*. I know that's a big promise but I tend to live by the axiom that you go big or you go home. If you're thinking you don't need this, let me ask you a question. If your marriage trends the way it's currently going for the next 10 years, do you expect to still be married? Will your marriage be meeting the expectations you had at the altar? Will your sex life with your spouse be better than ever? Will you crave to experience your mate physically, mentally and spiritually? Will your children be inspired by your example?

By now, I can only imagine what you are thinking. Hopefully it's either "This guy's off his rocker and I'm going to keep reading because I'm curious" or "I'm really inspired and excited because I'm ready to make a quantum leap in my relationship and my life". Hopefully it's the latter because you're about to gain access to powerful concepts that could change your life forever.

But before we go on, there is one thing you've got to bring to the table to make this happen—commitment. You've got to be committed to moving onward and upward. You've got to be committed to growing yourself as a human being and putting away childish things. You've got to be committed to pushing past limits that have stymied you in the past. You've got to be committed to forgetting the past and living in the present and for the future. You've got to be committed to yourself, to being the best YOU that you can be. You've got to be committed to giving 100%. That's what you deserve and that's what your mate deserves. See ACTION STEPS at the end of this chapter for a link to your commitment contract with yourself.

As you take this journey, you will be offered the opportunity to become the best you that you can be. Remember to allow that same gift to your mate. Don't see them through the eyes of who you think they are, but instead as the blossoming rose that they are becoming. Remember, change happens in a moment—the moment a decision is made to be different. And even though they may have acted consistent with their ideals, beliefs and values for as long as you've known them, they too will be challenged in unexpected ways. You will only hinder this process by responding, reacting and reinforcing who they have been, instead of what they are now, or are becoming.

We challenge you to become playful, resourceful and keep your focus on what you ultimately want to accomplish from reading this book. It only takes one shift in how you view your spouse, your marriage, or yourself to change the quality of your marriage for a lifetime.

Oh, and one final note. I'm going to offer you a formula. A model, or framework if you will, that when embraced and implemented into your life will change everything. That said, there are certain things that you will gravitate towards. Missing ingredients that will resonate in a special way for you. So as you read, I want you to interpret and interpolate this information in whatever way is most beneficial for you. Notice I didn't say in whatever way is most comfortable. Use the ideas, principles and philosophies as a muse, inspiration and launching pad for having the relationship that you deserve. If you don't agree with something or have a hard time swallowing it, that's OK. Just don't get hung up on it and throw the baby out with the bath water. I believe that the laws of relationships are universal. However, Pareto's law (the 80/20 rule) seems to always prevail. With the extreme biological, chemical, and physiological diversity we seem to now have in the human race, perhaps only about 20% of the population will be open to the message. And of those 20%, only about 20% of them will have the level of consciousness to see, or the desire to do what it takes to have an inspiring relationship and an inspiring life. I believe you are one of them.

So that was all just an appetizer. Now, let's get into the meat and potatoes (or tofu and rice if you prefer) of a passionate, life-long love affair.

ACTION STEPS

1. Keep reading!
2. Go to RESOURCES at www.GreatMarriageGreatLife.com and download your "Commitment Contract." Fill it out. Go down to your bank and have your signature notarized. Hey, you've got to take this stuff seriously!
3. If you feel like you need additional motivation and support moving forward, go to www.GreatMarriageGreatLife.com and sign up for our Blog. Kimberly and I talk about everything from romance in a busy life, sex with your kids in the next room, to healthy cooking, fitness, motivation, making ancient grain bread and slow food. The fun thing is that we transparently share our own challenges and experiences, and how we negotiate them in almost real time.

THE 3 ELEMENTS

I just want to remind you that this book isn't about how to have a good marriage, it's about how to have a *great* marriage and a passionate marriage that endures the test of time.

So, this is how we're going to roll. Here's the BIG PICTURE where I'll conceptually reveal the *3 Elements* of the Great Marriage-Great Life Elixir. We'll follow that up by going deep into each of these. The first *Element* is **LOVE**. The second *Element* is **POLARITY**. And the third *Element* is **PERSONAL DEVELOPMENT**.

These *3 Elements* will be covered over multiple chapters within 3 separate sections of the book. Each of the chapters contain distinctions that could by themselves transform your relationship depending on your particular situation. For example, your marriage may have 2 of the *3 Elements* but be missing the 3rd. And when you bring the 3rd *Element* into your experience, everything could transform for you faster than you ever imagined and in ways that you never dreamed possible.

Superficially, you may think you have each of the *3 Elements* covered in your marriage only to discover that you have been delusional. I know that sounds harsh but if you have any pain, frustration or lack of fulfillment in your marriage, one or more of these areas is not developed or developing the way you need it to. In other words, if you don't have a dynamic, passionate and fulfilling marriage, something that you may have thought you had is obviously missing. Otherwise, you probably wouldn't be reading this book. Personally, Kimberly helps me see my delusions quite frequently and by frequently I mean almost daily! I owe her a lot for the patience and kindness she has shown while providing me the opportunity to be a better husband and a better man. Our dedication to each other; our awareness and understanding of the *3 Elements*; and our conscious daily decision to make sure all *3 Elements* are present keep our marriage dynamic, passionate and fulfilling.

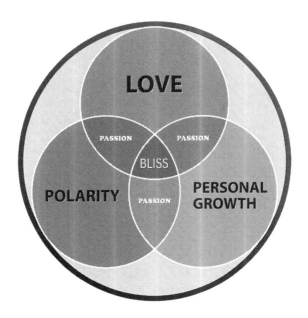

Note: You can print out a color PDF of the **3 Elements** for reference; to put in your journal, on your bed stand or hang on your refrigerator. The graphic is available under RESOURCES>DOWNLOADS at www.GreatMarriageGreatLife.com

LOVE (The 1st Element)

Love, love, love, love. I might as well say blah, blah, blah, blah. Love goes without saying, right? The last thing you probably think you need to read about is love. If that's where you're at, don't even think about skipping the section on love. I expect to give you some new perspectives on love that once understood may seem self-evident yet still leave your head spinning. If you are truly loving your mate, I mean loving them without condition and without limit; then your relationship is amazing, right? If people aren't asking you how you keep the "newlywed thing" going, something is missing in the love department. So we'll explore what it means to love and how simply keeping the promises you made at the altar can transform your marriage in months, weeks or even days. Because, if you want LOVE (the noun, the thing), you've got to learn how to LOVE (the verb, the action). Developing the capacity to love is the essence of human growth and spiritual development. Love truly is the answer. We just need to take a fresh look at it.

POLARITY (The 2nd Element)

Polarity in the context of relationship is the attraction that forms between a man and woman who have contrasting masculine and feminine energies. It's the natural electric tension that forms between 2 opposites that magnetizes them. How is polarity different than love and why is polarity important if you have love? Because you can love someone and not be attracted to them. It's a condition that is pandemic in marriages everywhere. Over time, attraction and desire for each other in long-term relationships wanes. It doesn't have to be that way. The problem is that if you don't have polarity, i.e., sexual attraction and desire for each other, it's obviously hard to have passion, rich conversation, fulfilling sex and in the long term it's difficult to want to stay together.

PERSONAL GROWTH (The 3rd Element)

Personal development plays a crucial role in a great marriage and a great life. Without it, one cannot love themselves completely; love their mates completely; nor can they maintain the polarity with their mate that ensures lasting sexual attraction and desire. I don't want to give it away yet but you will learn how personal growth plays a critical role in turning your marriage into a blissful flow experience. It's been mentioned at least a couple of times (and many more to come) that marriage is the perfect environment for personal growth. Well, not only does it offer the most consistent opportunity for growth, but personal development has a corresponding relationship to the capacity you have for love, passion and deep fulfillment.

Each one of the *3 Elements* plays a key role in the creation and support of a blissful and passionate marriage. You can have a "good" relationship with just 2 of the *Elements*, but good isn't good enough because it will never be as richly rewarding, deeply fulfilling, and spiritually enlightening as when you have all 3. And when you don't have all 3, you'll never experience the unshakeable certainty and freedom that comes with FULL-filled marriage. The *3 Elements* of LOVE, POLARITY and PERSONAL GROWTH can be likened to a *Sanctuary, Playground* and a *Classroom* respectively.

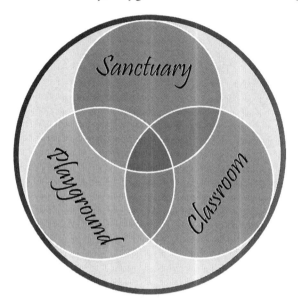

In what other relationship do we have the potential to experience and grow in love at a deep level; enjoy the fun, excitement, adventure of engaging with the opposite sex; and develop ourselves as human beings? Marriage is the ideal environment. It's our best shot at reaching our full potential. It's perfect!

So without further ado, let's dive in and start living the good life.

ACTION STEPS

1. Print out a color PDF of the **3 Elements** for reference, to put on your bed stand or hang on your refrigerator. The graphic is available under RESOURCES at www.GreatMarriageGreatLife.com

2. Print out the Sanctuary, Playground, Classroom graphic for your fridge. Personally, we love this illustration because it reminds us of how amazing marriage can be and where to keep our focus to keep it in balance. More on this later.

3. Commit to reading the next chapter.

WHY YOU *KNOW* WHAT TO DO, BUT DON'T DO IT

OK, I tricked you. We're not going to get into the *3 Elements* just yet. Here's why? Because I don't want to divulge to you the most profound secrets of the universe only to have you do NOTHING with them? What a shame that would be. It's been said that the greatest sin is knowing what to do but not having the gumption to do it. This condition of apathy, passivity and "un-resourcefulness" is pervasive amongst western civilization. It's what separates the 80-90% of those with mediocre and uninspiring lives from the 10-20% whose lives are rich, beaming with purpose and passion.

So why is it that we so often know what to do but just can't get ourselves to do it? Why is it that we can go to church, read self-help books, attend seminars, buy infomercial weight-loss programs and find ourselves in the very same place struggling with the same problems a year later? Why do most people make new year's resolutions that never come to fruition? I mean come on! We're all intelligent people, right?

Well, the answer to these questions isn't *resources*. It's *resourcefulness*. People who get what they want out of life, whether it be money, careers, peak health, physical fitness or amazing relationships, do so because they are more resourceful than their counterparts. As I see it, that resourcefulness manifests itself for 2 primary reasons.

First, resourceful people have leverage on themselves, meaning that they have a powerful *reason* to push beyond any pain or obstacles that might be standing between them and their desire. In other words, they have a BIG "why" that motivates them to do what they need to do even if it is uncomfortable.

Second, resourceful people learn to control their emotional states rather than allow their emotions to dictate their actions and behaviors. Everyone experiences the emotions of fear, anger, resentment, frustration, depression, sadness and apathy at some point. The difference is in learning to intentionally move out of these emotions into more empowered states that are in alignment with what we ultimately want in our relationships and our lives. Being able to control your emotional "state" of mind is one of the biggest, if not *the* biggest, determining factor for achieving what you want in life. And the state of your mind very often determines the quality of your relationship. In other words, the caliber of your thinking will govern or steer your relation-"ship". And ultimately, the quality of your relationship equals the quality of your life.

"...the caliber of your thinking will govern or steer your relation-"ship". And ultimately, the quality of your relationship equals the quality of your life."

Let's face it, sometimes you feel totally empowered and on top of the world and nothing can get you down. Other times you are not at your best and you just don't feel like being loving. You're impatient, overly sensitive, intolerant, easily riled and just seem to see everything through a muddy windshield. Even if the latter seems to be the norm for you now, everyone has experienced optimal states where nothing could get you down; where you could take on anything or you just seemed to see the comedy in everything instead of the dread. The only difference between a problem and an opportunity is simply the state in which you view it.

When you are in an empowered state, the minutia that would normally drive you crazy or get on your nerves just evaporate. And everyone to a large degree has the ability to manage if not determine their own state. How great would it be if you could always choose optimism over pessimism, gratitude over despair, resourcefulness over apathy, or excitement over dread? Well, you can! You are actually your own puppeteer. If you can't connect with that metaphor then try this one—you are your own dog. You are the dog and your emotional state is the tail.

Learning to manage your state is a crucial component of you getting what you want out of your marriage. It's the only way that you can consistently bring the best YOU to your relationship. And if you want your mate to be the best they can be, it really helps if you are the best you can be. In other words, if you want to manifest the husband or wife of your dreams, then be the person that the husband or wife of your dreams would be attracted to.

People say to Kimberly and me all the time that we must have something "special". They are implying that the love and passion we have for each other is atypical, not normal, and maybe even an anomaly. We can tell that they are trying to explain the contrast between what they have and what we have in our marriage, and do it in a way that excuses them from respon-

"...if you want to manifest the husband or wife of your dreams, then be the person that the husband or wife of your dreams would be attracted to."

sibility. To that I have to say that they are correct. We do have something "special". But that isn't to say that they can't have an extraordinary "special" relationship as well. Ordinary, normal, average marriages are just that— ordinary. They are that way because they are doing what ordinary, normal, average people do. And if you do what ordinary, normal, average people do, you'll get what ordinary, normal, average people get. Great marriages don't just happen. Extraordinary marriages happen because we've created an environment that encourages, fosters and promotes them.

"Extraordinary marriages happen because we've created an environment that encourages, fosters and promotes them."

People who are the epitome of health, live a lifestyle utilizing whole natural foods, body movement and spiritual wellbeing to create a physical environment that produces energy and vitality. Likewise, couples with outstanding marriages have created an environment of love, polarity and differentiation (we'll get into this later) that fosters passion and deep connection. Those "lucky few" that have that "special" relationship have it because they do what most others don't.

This chapter is about getting yourself to do what you want to do and need to do, to take action and, consequently, your marriage to a new level. You can read every marriage book and go to every couples retreat out there, but if you can't get yourself to execute and apply what you've learned, what's the point, right?

So the first thing you need is a powerful "WHY"? The WHY is the compelling reason that will get you to do what you know you should do; get you to move beyond your self-imposed limitations; and provide you the deep purpose and meaning behind it all. The WHY is what will drive you, compel you and inspire you to learn, stretch and grow as a human being. The WHY will compel you to discard bad habits, inspire you to build emotional muscle, and motivate you to learn to love at a deeper level. Oh, and did I mention that personal growth is really what this is all about?

The Why of the Why

Why do we do what we do? The first answer is that we want to be happy. We get married to be happy and we get divorced to be happy. We get up early to be happy and we sleep in late to be happy. We go to college to be happy and we avoid college to be happy. Women with straight hair curl it to be happy and those with naturally curly hair often go to great lengths to straighten it. We work out in the gym to be happy and we eat ice cream to be happy.

However, lasting happiness is much more a choice than a result of what we do, get or have. It's a state of mind that we can evoke at will if we understand the components of how to achieve, create and live "happiness". More on this later.

The second reason we do what we do is to avoid pain. In fact, we'll often go to more trouble to avoid pain than we ever would to be happy. Pain is a huge motivator. Some people will go to college to avoid the pain of poverty rather than the pleasure of financial independence. I know people who eat an extremely healthy diet to avoid the pain of disease rather than enjoy the pleasure of good health. Some of us go to work to avoid the pain of being thrown out on the street. Some of us go to work to avoid the pain of being at home with our spouse. Historically, the fear of pain was used by the church to coerce the masses into subscribing to its doctrine.

Pleasure and pain are tools to be used to help you get what you want in your life. Since you are always attempting to move away from pain and move towards pleasure or happiness, you can use this inherent desire to compel you to the marriage you want and the life you want. So why is it that we so often can't get ourselves to do what we want to do or know we should do? It's because we don't have a big enough WHY. We don't have a reason that's compelling enough to get us to move off dead center. We either don't associate enough pleasure with taking action and making the change or we don't associate enough pain with NOT taking action and making the change. In other words, we don't have any leverage on ourselves.

Most everyone who achieves extraordinary things has leverage on themselves. In the context of marriage, most people don't do what they know they need to do to have a great relationship because a) they don't comprehend the pain they will experience by not doing it, b) they don't comprehend the joy, pleasure and happiness they will experience if they do it, c) they associate too much pain with changing their own behavior, or d) they are getting their own personal needs met (albeit at a primitive level) without having to change.

On a practical level, the way to use pain and pleasure to get yourself to take action is to associate enormous pleasure, joy and happiness with achieving your goal and associate a massive amount of pain, agony and distress with not achieving your goal. Imagine what your life will be like when you are the man or woman that the man or woman of your dreams is attracted to. What will it be like when your time together is the most rewarding part of your day? How will it feel to be romanced and pursued? How will it feel when you can't wait to see each other again? How deeply meaningful, passionate and erotic will your sex life be? How will this affect and influence your children and your children's children? Your greater family? Your community? How will this benefit your health? Your longevity? Now, let me ask you this: What will your life be like if you maintain status quo? What will it look like if you take the divorce route? What pain will it cause you? What pain will it cause your mate? How detrimental will it be to your children? If you don't transform your marriage by being the best you can be, what example is that going to leave for your children? What emotional traumas might they carry with them the rest of their lives? How might your selfishness, complacency or apathy be affecting your health or worse your mate's health? Is your unwillingness to grow, change and evolve as a human being causing those you love harm? By the way, there is no status quo. You are either growing your relationship or you are inadvertently strangling it, smothering it or poisoning it. I know that sounds harsh but it's true.

Now, the questions just asked are tough questions. These are my questions. These are the very questions I asked myself 17 years ago (and still ask) to build up a big enough WHY to get leverage on myself. What is your WHY?

One most likely seeks out a book like this because they've reached a threshold of pain that pushed them to make a change.

However, be conscious of how pain motivates you and how when it begins to subside, you often lose your motivation.

An example of this would be one's desire to lose 10 pounds as a New Year's resolution. The inspiration may come from the pain of not being able to button your pants or seeing some cellulite in the mirror. You go on a diet and lose enough to see results. What happens then? The pain subsides and you stop doing what you did to get the results until, once again, the pain pendulum tips and you make a new resolution.

The problem with "New Year's Resolution Syndrome" is that it's like yo-yo dieting. If you don't have a strong enough "why" or driving force behind your efforts, they aren't sustainable.

Emotional Mastery

Whether you know it or not, you have the ability to massively influence yourself, your mate and consequently the state of your marriage. You can exert this influence solely through your emotional state. I'm not talking about Norman Vincent Peale's *Power of Positive Thinking* here, although that's part of it. What I'm talking about is learning to put yourself into an optimal frame of mind so that you're in the driver's seat of your life and your circumstances begin to bend to your will. This is the second part of the "How do I get myself to do what I know I should do?" question.

When I earlier proposed that we do what we do to be happy, another way it could have been said is that we do what we do to feel good. We all know what it's like to feel good. When you feel good, life is good. When you feel good, you are unstoppable. When you feel good, you are more resourceful. Your ability to bring your best to the table in your marriage is at a high.

On the flipside, when you feel like crap, what happens? Your resourcefulness is diminished, your patience is low, your capacity to love is diminished, your enthusiasm for meeting your mate's needs evaporates, and your attitude might suck. How important do you think it is to feel good in your marriage? Well, when you feel good, you are good. And when you are good, you do good.

Feeling good is your responsibility. You can't sit around waiting for the planets to align to feel good. You've got to live your life on purpose and with intention and you've got to approach your marriage with purpose and intention. After all, it is heaven's gift to you to help you grow in your divinity and bless your life with deep enjoyment, fulfillment and meaning.

Being in a positive, resourceful state is likened to having your A-game turned on. Every top performer in business, sports, or entertainment has the ability to get themselves into state before they enter their arena. Tennis players like Rafael Nadal, Novak Djokovic and Roger Federer are phenomenal tennis players. They definitely know *how* to play tennis. But that's not why they win so much. They consistently perform at a high level because they have a superior psychology. They've mastered the ability to apply what they know in the most challenging circumstances. In other words, they've mastered the ability to muster a high state of physical energy and emotional strength at will.

So how does this specifically apply to your marriage? Well, for starters, if your state is high and your mate's state is high, the quality of your relationship will be high. If you both have low states, the quality of your experience will be low. If your state is high and theirs is low, your job is to throw them a "lifesaver" and help them raise their state to a higher level and so on. Whatever you expect from your mate, you will look for evidence to support your expectations. In other words, if you think your mate is a bitch/bastard and approach the day thinking, "I wonder what bitchy or jerky thing they're going to say today", all you're going to see is anything that you can construe to support your expectation. We see what we expect to see. We find what we are looking for. We manifest what we are directing our energy towards. If our state is strong enough, we will bring those around us up to our level or down to it as the case may be. Our state determines what we expect. If we are optimistic, we look for the good in everything. And what will we find? The good! If you want the wife/husband of your dreams, then act like they are the wife/husband of your dreams expecting the results you want.

Labelling a person can so powerfully influence their future performance. When teachers label kids with learning disabilities e.g., "highly intelligent", "disadvantaged", "lazy", "mischievous" or "sensitive", it can affect how that child grows or regresses as they progress through school.

This point was emphasized in the movie based on a true story, Seabiscuit. The lead character trains a horse with incredible ability that was previously used to build the self-confidence of other race horses by intentionally losing races against them. Once the trainer identifies what motivates the horse, he goes from being an average training horse to a national hero, winning many horse races.

Sometimes we only need someone to believe in us, see us better than we are, and treat us as if we are already that person. When you treat your mate as highly intelligent, funny, sweet and creative, you can evoke the best of their abilities. Humans often rise or fall to the expectations of their peers. Why not see a masterpiece in the making? Think of your mate as your hero, your lover, your collaborator, your confidant, your best friend, and beckon the traits that come with each.

I've been told by other marriage advocates that the key to a happy marriage is low expectations, and while I understand how that can help a marriage on some level, I offer a different perspective. I have extremely high expectations of my mate and my marriage. It's impossible for any human being to always rise to the challenge but I find that my view of what my husband is capable of, cultivates an environment where we both bring our best to the occasion, most of the time.

How to Access A Quality State

Personal development coach, Tony Robbins, teaches the importance of learning to master your state, and I thank him for introducing me to the concept many years ago. There are 3 primary things that determine your state at any given time whether you realize it or not. I have personally tested and proven these things to be responsible for any state you are experiencing excepting those induced by trauma, drugs or a medical condition outside your control. The 3 components of state are focus, physiology and meaning. I will explain each component of the State Trifecta in further detail as they relate to how you feel at any given time.

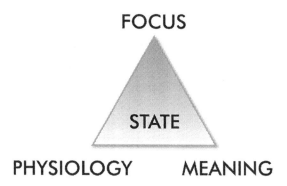

Component 1: Focus

Whatever we focus on seems to manifest in our lives. Whatever we give attention to grows and becomes a dominant part of our experience. Your focus is what you are concentrating on with your physical eyes and your mind's eye. It's what you think about consistently. If you focus on what's beautiful about your mate, that's what you will see and respond to. If you focus on the bad habits and defects of your mate, they will dominate your perception of that person.

Focusing on what you have control over in your life empowers you to make a difference. Focusing on what is outside your control like your partner's character flaws will drive you crazy, make you reactionary, and bring out the worst in you. When you look for the good in a situation, you'll find it. If you look for what stinks, you'll always find something that stinks even if you have to subconsciously manufacture it. This, by the way, is something that we do to feel congruent. Whatever you believe to be true *is* true for you. If you hold onto a belief that it's your spouse's fault that your marriage is in shambles, you'll find ample evidence to support the belief. To the contrary, if you hold the belief that there are good qualities in your mate and you focus on those, the stimulus response dynamic between you will change for the good.

If you think about what is beautiful in your life and everything you have to be thankful for, you'll experience the emotion of gratitude. Gratitude sure feels better than resentment. Always remember that an attitude of gratitude raises your altitude. In fact, it's difficult to experience any negative emotions when you are in a state of gratitude. This distinction by itself is transformational because it gives you a practice that you can implement anytime, anywhere to change your state and your perspective. Sitting down together as a couple and sharing what you are grateful for is both empowering and connecting. Now that's something to be grateful for, don't you think?

Another powerful type of focus is experienced through prayer and meditation. Stay tuned, I don't want to lose you on this one because it is really fascinating. A contemporary way of describing the power of prayer and meditation is in using the words "focused intention." The underlying message in the book *The Secret,* is that you will manifest in your life whatever you focus on with congruence. In other words, when you align your focus, your thoughts, your intentions, and your actions to the same outcome or desire, the pieces to your puzzle seem to fall together effortlessly. I don't know about the "effortlessly" part, but I can tell you with certainty that when your focus, intention and actions are all in alignment, your congruence generates an energy that attracts the object of your intention into your life.

Praying for yourself or others has always been a faith-based practice with an efficacy largely unexplainable. Recent research has shown that not only can prayer and intention significantly affect your own health, wellbeing and behavior, but also that of others. Participants in a study in Hawaii were all hooked up to functional magnetic resonance imaging (fMRI) in an isolated environment. On a schedule unknown to the participant, spiritual healers would send prayers and focused intention for the wellbeing of the participant. According to the scans, at precisely the same times that the participants were being prayed for or focused on with positive intention, certain areas of their brains would activate.

The only insight I want you to take from this is the possibility that your mate is influenced by your feelings, your thoughts, and your intentions whether you are in their presence or not. Being in an empowered and loving state toward your spouse is imperative even when you're not with them. They will subconsciously pick up on it, and it will predispose their feelings and behavior toward you before you even have a chance to get your foot in the door. The message? Deeply focus on your mate for moments throughout the day. Send them your love as if in a prayer. Not only will this help set their emotional stage for a more loving reception, but it will also help you maintain a lovingly empowered state. Think of it as a pre-shot routine. Golfers and tennis players all have pre-shot routines. It's the routine series of motions they go through prior to striking or serving the ball. These rituals set them up for success by helping them get present, focused and intent on the outcome that they want in that moment.

I've noticed how women enjoy sharing their problems with friends; almost to the point that the monthly book club meeting becomes venting hour. I make an effort and recommend only speaking highly of your mate and avoid talking about their so-called "faults", past wrongdoings and current complaints to others. In general, unless you're speaking to someone that has a good marriage and you're sharing with the intention of gleaning good advice to implement, it will only add fuel to the fire. Girlfriends tend to sympathize with you, and support your viewpoint that your mate should change, or how wrong they were, or what action you should take, while making these judgments and decisions in a disempowered state.

Your test will come when your mate is acting like a bitch or an ass and your attention is now focused on their offensive behavior. I find it helpful in these acutely appalling moments to recall "my stack". What is a stack? It's a stack of fond memories—great experiences I've had with this person. After all, if I stopped and thought about it I would recognize that he's not acting from his highest and best self. Clearly his attention has been misdirected from a place of gratitude to the gutter.

The best way to create your stack, is to journal life's best memories. Write them down as they occur. I write down not only magical moments but treasured comments my mate makes that remind me how much I mean to him, how he adores me and why he has chosen me to be his one and only for life.

The Power of Questions

The questions we ask ourselves can determine our focus. Thinking is not much more than the internal process of asking and answering questions. Here are examples of benign questions that probably won't impact your state one way or the other:

- Should I take a shower?
- What should I wear?
- This belt or that?
- Breakfast at home or on the run?
- I wonder what's for dinner?
- I wonder when daylight savings time starts?
- I wonder if we're going to have sex tonight? (On second thought, if

you have to wonder this too often, your state will probably deteriorate as a result.)

Here are examples of disempowering questions that will negatively affect your state. These questions predispose you to negativity and un-resourcefulness. Negative questions yield negative answers. If you're looking for answers in your life, you certainly don't want the answers to the following questions showing up. Whatever you focus on seems to show up consistently whether you like it or not. Be careful of questions like these:

- Is my boss going to pressure me today?
- Is my wife going to be the usual nag she always is?
- When should I start a diet?
- Why does this always happen to me?
- Why is it always someone else getting the raise?
- Why don't I ever win the lottery?
- What's my husband's problem?
- Why do my kids hate me?
- Why don't I have enough money?
- Why did that jerk cut me off?
- I wonder if I'm going to hit it in the water like always?

These questions put your mind in the gutter because if you look for thistles you will find thistles. If you look for roses you'll find roses. Your choice.

Now let's take a look at some empowering questions. By empowering, I mean questions that elevate your thinking. Questions that result in answers that provide tools to get what you want. Questions that tap into your resourcefulness. Questions that make you feel good just by asking them. Questions like:

- What can I do today to make my mate feel more loved?
- What is within my power to make a difference in the environment?
- What 3 things could I do today to boost the quality of my marriage?
- What could I do to double my income in the next year?
- How can I capitalize on my unique skills to make some extra money?
- What unique opportunities are there in this recession?
- What one thing could I do today to move closer to my fitness goals?

- What do I love most about my children?
- What are 3 things I'd like to change in my life, and what single step can I take today toward that change?
- If I could make my living doing anything I wanted, what would it be?
- How did I get so lucky to have this person in my life?

Notice how these questions affect your physiology just reading them. Do you feel yourself breathing deeper, maybe holding your head higher? How about your face? Does it feel a little more relaxed? Isn't this the way to think? Can you see the track we're on here? Never focus on what you don't want in your life. Focus only on what you want, on the goal, on the ideal. Focus only on what you are grateful for in your life and on new possibilities. Slip on some metaphorical rose-colored glasses and remember what you love about the person you married. Now that's what I'm talking about!

Component 2: Physiology

Physiology is the study of the relationship of all your bodily systems to one another. In this context we could call it your physical self. What you do with your body directly affects how you feel. Your posture, movement or lack thereof, facial expressions and depth of breath, all affect how you feel. Did you know that it's almost impossible to feel depressed when you have good posture, breathe deeply, and move around quickly with a smile on your face? Try it next time you feel low. You'll pick yourself right up. If you look closely at anyone who's depressed, what do you see? You see slumped shoulders, shallow breathing, and eyes to the floor.

If you notice your own physiology when you feel on top of the world. You see that you have good posture, your head is held up high, and you move around with intention. Tennis is my favorite sport to illustrate the relationship between emotional state and physiology. I saw a match between Americans, James Blake and Andy Roddick. I think it was the third set with Blake down 2 sets and starting to lose ground in the third. You could see his attitude deteriorating along with his physiology. His shoulders had dropped, his face looked defeated, and he started walking more slowly. You could see him beating himself up, and the more he beat up on himself, the worse he played. Then something really cool happened. The crowd got behind him and started cheering him on. The crowd's energy lifted his spirits, broke his disempowering state, and inspired him to play his all-out best. He turned the game around, won the third set, and kept the match going. I think he eventually lost but did it with dignity.

The question in my mind is, what came first for Blake? Did he first change what he was thinking or did he first change what he was doing? In other words, did his demeanor influence his emotional state or did his new emotional state influence his demeanor? Strange question? We've known now for a long time how our minds can affect our bodies. We often call it the mind-body connection. It's been proven beyond any doubt by countless studies that what's going on in your mind directly impacts your body's chemistry, biological processes and physical health in general. What the mind imagines, the body manifests. But what about the other way around? To what extent does what we do with our bodies actually affect our minds?

The Botox Connection

I recently learned the term "embodied cognition". In simple terms (I like simple terms) cognition is the processes of the mind. Embodied cognition suggests that your mental processes are influenced and shaped by everything going on in your body.

The most astounding example of this is the discovery that our facial expressions are hardwired to our emotions. This means that we can't have an emotion without a facial expression and we can't have a facial expression without a corresponding emotion. Am I the only one who thinks this is cool? This means that we can influence how we feel by simply changing the expressions on our faces. So if you want to feel happy, ladies, you've got to embrace the crow's feet at the corners of your eyes. Crow's feet are smile wrinkles. Real heart-felt smiles cause the muscles in your cheeks to contract and consequently the skin at the corner of your eyes to crinkle. They also make you feel better.

The even more astounding finding is the effect of Botox on your capacity to experience emotions. Studies have shown that people injected with Botox have difficulty experiencing the emotions normally associated with certain facial expressions. For example, subjects who received Botox injections in their frown lines were often relieved of depression because they could no longer frown. Other Botox recipients found that their ability to empathize with others greatly diminished. I don't know about you but I'm going to exercise my power of choice and choose to embody facial expressions that support the emotions I want to experience. And as for Botox, I'm going to call and cancel my appointment right now!

Kimberly and I went to our first Tony Robbins event in the late '90s. One of the many extraordinary things we took away with us was the ability to influence our state using what Tony referred to as a "power move". If you don't have your own power move you've certainly seen someone do one when they felt a peak emotion. It's something that most people might associate with sports. Two examples of this are the fist pump after sinking a tough putt in a golf tournament or the ritualistic celebration dance after making a touchdown in a football game. The significance of these moves is not just celebratory but that they also serve to anchor intensely empowering states with the physiology associated with "the move". In other words, your nervous system learns that when you do *this*, you're supposed to feel like *that*.

The obvious benefit to this is that you can quickly work yourself into an empowered state by simply doing your power move. To be able to do this, you first develop the neuro-association to the move by repeatedly doing your power move (whatever that might be), while you are in a peak emotional state. Then, just like with the facial expression/emotional connection, you "hardwire" a connection between your emotions and your power move.

There's another way to do this that's more organic. As in the case with the Botox Connection, our minds naturally respond to body movement and stature. I recently watched a TED talk by psychologist Amy Cuddy entitled *Your body language may shape who you are,* where she emphasized that not only do our minds change our bodies but our bodies change our minds. You've probably heard the catch-phrase "fake it 'til you make it". It means act as if something is true until it becomes true. An example of this is choosing to act like you're an experienced public speaker even if you're not. Why would you do this? Because if you're terrified of public speaking, you will probably never do it. However, if you "fake it 'til you make it", act as if, or pretend that you love public speaking—in other words, you do what a confident public speaker does—you will manifest the physiology and psychology of an experienced public speaker.

In the context of your relationship where you need to feel empowered to be the best friend and lover your mate has, physiologically acting as if you are those things helps bring them into reality. Learn to embody the physical expressions, movements and statures of the personas that you want to authentically bring to your relationship when you are at your best.

I think of this as my Recipe for Success and Empowerment. When you can identify the characteristics of how you're moving, feeling and thinking when you're at your best, you have your RECIPE for an empowering state.

During a recent Ted Talk interview, Serena Williams commented how she emulates the BEST. Think about the characteristics of someone you most admire and why. Try to identify what they do emotionally, physically and mentally that helps them produce their results. Becoming a new version of you can simply be the result of acting like the person that you want to be. In this context, I'm not talking about acting like someone else. I'm talking about acting out your own highest and best version of yourself.

For a woman this may be embodying her feminine attributes and strengths in the way she stands, sits, walks, smiles and talks. This helps her live and communicate from her true essence giving her confidence and self-assurance, not forgetting that it makes her magnetizing.

For a man, standing, sitting, walking and communicating in a way that exemplifies confidence, control and inner strength facilitates the manifestation of those very traits not to mention they nurture his masculinity. Learn to consistently be aware of your physiology and make adjustments that are in alignment with who you want to be, for yourself and for your mate.

The Health Connection

Another significant aspect of physiology is your general state of health. If you're not healthy, it's hard to feel good. If you don't feel good, it's hard to be in a good state. If you're overweight, you can't move with spring in your step. If you don't get enough sleep, not only will you be dragging your tail around, but your emotional fuse will be shorter and your ability to focus compromised. If you don't take care of yourself physically with a healthy diet and exercise routine, it's impossible to be your best; it's impossible to meet the demands of life. Think about it, if you are tired all the time, how can you maintain a healthy and vibrant sex life? Being too tired to have sex isn't a reason to not have sex. It's a reason to reassess your values and reprioritize your life. Meaning, you need to take better care of yourself for you and the ones you love. If you're grumpy, impatient, and short-fused all the time, maybe you're sleep deprived and it's time to reevaluate the stressors in your life and make some new quality decisions. Or maybe you need to change your pre-bed routine to something that quiets your mind.

Have you noticed how difficult it is to feel in a peak emotional state when you're sick, tired or physically injured? The foundation for emotional mastery is how you feel physically. We need to assess our overall health and consider the little things that help us harness maximum energy like quality sleep, effective exercise and overall physical vitality. You owe it to yourself and your mate to create a body that functions at optimal performance—taking time for daily exercise (even 20 minutes a day can pay huge dividends for our health); adequate water intake to hydrate and alkalize our bodies (a lack of which can make us tired and sluggish); nutrient dense foods not processed by man (think whole foods such as fruits, vegetables in their natural state, and organic meats); and quality sleep which can be aided by a consistent pre-bedtime routine, no computers after dinner, an evening stroll to relax and unwind, and allowing the recommended nightly allowance of 8-10 hours per night for adults.

If your diet includes a lot of unhealthy fats and sugars, this can affect your energy levels and your emotions. Since this book isn't about diet, I'm not going to mention the disastrous effects of eating foods containing refined sugars, refined flours, artificial sweeteners and trans fats. If you haven't seen any already, there are a plethora of food documentaries available on Netflix and iTunes that reveal disturbing but real facts about how the aforementioned foods are pandemically affecting the rise of obesity, diabetes, heart disease and ADHD. Three such films that come to mind are *Super Size Me, That SUGAR Film,* and *Forks over Knives.*

Ah shucks, did I just mention diet? Can't help myself. In 2015, Forbes published an article stating that nearly 50% of all Americans either had diabetes or were pre-diabetic. That is shocking to say the least. That is evidence that America is addicted to junk food and it's killing them. Meanwhile, the National Institute of Diabetes and Digestive and Kidney Diseases says that over two-thirds of adult Americans are either overweight or obese. Do you think you can live up to your potential when you're suffering the symptoms and side effects of excess weight, disease, insomnia and emotional disorders? I haven't yet mentioned the detrimental effects of sedentary living on your energy levels and vitality. Did you know that?

Component 3: Meaning

The meaning that we give something is greatly influenced by the language we use both internally and externally. By language, I mean how you express yourself, and the vocabulary you use. The way you describe things to yourself or others often becomes your reality of those things.

For me, this is very powerful because it demonstrates another area of control that I have over my reality. The only truth your brain knows and responds to is what you tell it. For example, if you got a flat tire on the way home and you describe your day as being "ruined," how are you going to feel? How will you likely respond to other drivers on the road? What kind of state are you bringing home to your family? How different would it feel if you described the experience as "interesting" or "enlightening," as in "Gee, I didn't know how hard it was to get the spare tire out from underneath the car!" or if you're a guy, "Good thing that happened to me and not my wife. I better do a how-to-change-a-tire workshop at home so she can handle it if it ever happens to her."

When someone cuts you off in traffic, how do you respond? Do you say "Wow, that was close" or do you say "What a jerk" and flip them the bird? Can you guess which statement leaves you in a more pleasant state? If the last thing you said to someone was "What a jerk", how do you think your first interaction with the next person in line will be? If you say to yourself that you "never" have sex anymore, whether true or not, "never" will become a self-fulfilling prophecy. Do you have "devastating" experiences in your life on a daily basis? Or is life "great" no matter what happens?

What you say consistently does become a self-fulfilling prophecy, because your words translate into actions and your mate will respond accordingly.

When I was a kid, my grandfather *Pappy* lovingly reprimanded me when someone asked me how I was and I answered with something like "Fine, thank you." He would say, "When someone asks you how you are, you tell them that you are "GREAT! and you say it with emphasis." I now know how wise he was. It always put me in a better state and made me feel bigger than I really was. What kind of a sniveling response is "fine" or "okay"? Here's a list of words you might consider incorporating into your communications with yourself and others. They make you feel good just saying them.

Awesome	Delicious	Super	Wealth
Great	Dynamic	Abundance	Sexy
Perfect	Exceptional	Breakthrough	Nutritious
Amazing	Solutions	Brilliant	Magic
Beautiful	Outstanding	Epiphany	Fascinating

Now here's a list of example words to avoid using. They can get you feeling depressed or at least disempowered in a heartbeat.

Can't	Devastating	Hopeless	Lousy
Won't	Ruined	Bitch	Sick
Should	Afraid	Disaster	Okay
Could	No	Terrible	Stressed
Hate	Suffer	Failure	Worried

These words suck! Don't allow them into your thoughts or conversations. Get in the habit of censoring your thoughts and words. There are alternative ways to describe your thoughts and experiences that are more empowering. Like my Pappy used to say, "If you can't say something positive, don't say anything at all."

The HAPPY Formula

In his book *Flow*, Mihaly Csikszentmihalyi stated that "[happiness] does not depend on outside events, but rather, on how we interpret them… People who learn to control inner experience will be able to determine the quality of their lives, which is as close as any of us can come to being happy". The inner experience Mihaly is referring to is determined by what we focus on, the meaning we give what we're focusing on, and the actions we take as a result.

As stated earlier, our thoughts are essentially a constant stream of questions. The answers we conjure up in response to these questions determine the meaning of what we are focusing on and to a large extent our state. We're constantly looking for meaning in everything—the tone of someone's voice, the look on their face, the fact that someone didn't call you, the fact that you weren't invited to someone's party, or the job promotion that was given to someone else. What did that mean? Each one of these examples could mean that someone didn't like you, snubbed you, forgot about you, insulted you or thought you were incompetent. Or the meanings could have been that they were just thinking of someone else, they were being stung by a bee, they were in pain, they had temporary memory loss, or maybe they have a bigger promotion in mind for you if you show enough emotional maturity while seemingly being passed over.

Your reality is the reality of your inner experience and your inner experience is whatever you make of it. If we're going to assign a meaning to something, why not compose a meaning that supports an empowering state? And yes, you just lost the rationale to blame your mate for how you feel. *You* determine how you feel by how you internally respond to external circumstances. How you feel often determines how you act and how you consistently act will determine your ability to realize that which you desire. Tony Robbins says "It is in your moments of decision that your destiny is shaped". In other words, it's the choices that you make that determine your future whether it be the body you have in the future, the health you have in the future, the career that you have in the future or the marriage that you have in the future.

Curiously, individuals often question whether they married the right person, thinking that they are up against 50/50 odds of choosing the right person. I'll tell you right now that the success of your marriage has nothing to do with statistical probability. Divorce statistics merely reflect historical divorce rates but don't serve whatsoever in predicting the probability of success in anyone's marriage. Whether you have a passionate, fulfilling, meaningful and enduring marriage is determined by the choices you make every day.

The really cool thing about choices is that they can bring you back to the track you want to be on even after making poor ones. It's kind of like following a road map to a chosen destination. Along the way, you are faced with many crossroads and forks in the road. Sometimes we make wrong choices, take the wrong road and get off track. But as soon as we recognize that we've messed up, we make corrections (choices) to get us back on the desired route. So, choose to choose, and choose well. Your marriage destiny is in your hands.

ACTION STEPS

1. Remember, getting what you want out of your relationship or your life isn't about resources. It's all about resourcefulness. If you want something badly enough, there is always a way and it starts with you taking 100% responsibility for being where you are, and for getting where you want to go.

2. How do you rate your health, vitality and energy? List the 3 most important things you could start today to improve your health and take action right now to incorporate the most important one into your life. Then make a plan to incorporate the last 2 over the next 2 months.

3. Consider how many times you've seen that rare couple that just seems to have it all together and how you may have said to yourself, "Gee, they sure have something special." We do this to acknowledge what we see, but sometimes also to rationalize away what we don't have. Don't forget that couples who have "special" relationships do so because they consistently do special things. Come up with 3 special things that you can do right now that would make your mate feel more loved, honored and respected, and commit to doing them in the next 24 hours.

4. Behind every great accomplishment is a compelling "why". What is your compelling why? This is the reason that you must do whatever is in your power to take your marriage from where it is to where you want it to be.

5. The quality of your marriage will largely be determined by the quality of your emotional state. Use your Focus, Physiology and Meaning to control how you feel. Getting mastery over your inner experience is the secret to living a quality life.

6. Download the State Trifecta graphic image under RESOURCES at www.GreatMarriageGreatLife.com

SECTION 1:
LOVE

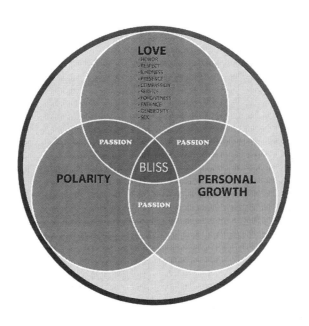

LOVE
- HONOR
- RESPECT
- KINDNESS
- PRESENCE
- COMPASSION
- SERVICE
- FORGIVENESS
- PATIENCE
- GENEROSITY
- SEX

PASSION   PASSION

BLISS

POLARITY   PERSONAL
GROWTH

PASSION

LOVE IS THE ANSWER

WEDDINGS. I LOVE WEDDINGS. Two people meet; there's an animal magnetism or peculiar spark of interest; they look for signs that the object of their attraction is a suitable mate; nature's species-preservation cocktail of dopamine, norepinephrine and oxytocin starts trickling in, enhancing their desire for each another and their bond to one another. That lovin' feeling is intoxicating and by golly they don't want to lose it. So they attempt to obtain certainty by getting married—certainty that they won't lose this person who is so integral to the feelings of love, excitement, and significance that they have when they're with them. They'll promise anything, and even mean it. They just naively don't give much thought to what it is they're really promising and their implications.

Marriage vows, a lot like "love", are so mundane, ordinary and routine, that they are practically a cliché. I can say this because if they were anything but, there would be little to no divorce in this country. Please forgive me if this statement doesn't apply to you but can you remember your vows? Have you consistently honored them? Do you begin your day with the intention to be faithful to your mate in every way that you promised? Seems like a no-brainer, right? Well, before you get upset with me over any implication that you have been unfaithful to your wedding vows, just hear me out.

So what the heck did we promise to do at the altar anyway? I know I never really thought about it again until after Kimberly and I had been married about 15 years. I'm a little bewildered about that to say the least. All I cared about at the time was getting the girl. I would have promised anything! So, here we go...

There are 2 categories of promises that you made at the altar. **Explicit Vows** (the promises that you verbally made) and **Implicit Vows** (the promises that you may not have consciously or verbally made but your beloved fairly presumed you were making). WHAT???

Stay with me here because I am about to reveal to you the primary reason why people lose attraction for each other, why infidelity often happens, and why marriages fail.

Explicit Vows

Explicit vows are the promises you made in the words that you spoke and/ or agreed to when you got married. They typically included promises to love, to honor, to cherish, to be faithful, etc. This is all boilerplate stuff, right? The problem with boilerplate language is that we take it for granted and it tends to lose its significance over time. So let me ask you, what does it mean to love, honor, cherish and be faithful? This is where we get into Implicit Vows.

Implicit Vows

Implicit vows are promises that are implied. When you promised to love, to honor and to cherish your beloved, they presumed that you would meet their needs faithfully without question, without fight, without controversy, and without delay. That is why you got married; to help guarantee that the feelings, emotions and experiences that you were having together during courtship would not go away. You got married so that you could have certainty; emotional certainty and sexual certainty.

Here's the rub. People often have no conscious idea or plan for meeting their mate's emotional needs. Most people don't even know what their mate's emotional needs are. And if they do, they shrug them off because they're not congruent with their own needs. For example, guys often don't understand a woman's need for consistent unsexual attention any more than women understand a guy's need for unemotional sexual connection and release. Sometimes we acknowledge these things on a superficial level but fail to consistently honor them because they don't fit our own personal model or hierarchy of needs. We also forget that we actually, explicitly or implicitly, promised to meet these needs, for better or for worse. The promise wasn't conditional.

I want to qualify the aforementioned example by saying that as a couple's experience together grows in the *3 Elements* explained in this book, their sexuality as a couple will evolve into something that transcends the familiar and very typical stereotype in the example above.

Generally speaking, men and women get married for the following reasons.

(This is by no means a comprehensive list. There are other reasons people get married that are far less virtuous.) These are in no particular order.

Why Men Get Married (Ladies, I'm talking to you)

1. Because you make him feel significant. Every man needs to be a hero and marrying you grants him permanent hero status. At least it gives him a tangible opportunity to be a hero on an ongoing basis.
2. Because he needs certainty about having consistent and gratifying sex.
3. Because he wants certainty that no one else will get you.
4. Because you make him feel good and he doesn't want that feeling to go away.
5. Because the way you look, feel, smell, behave, and interact with him in a way that attracts him, tantalizes him and makes him want you and love you.
6. Because you make him feel wanted and worthy of having.
7. Your femininity supports his masculinity. Your feminine softness and vulnerability support his need to feel like a provider and protector.
8. Because he is in love with being in love.
9. Because he is out of his mind. Just kidding!

Why Women Get Married (Gentlemen, I'm talking to you)

1. Because she wants to have certainty about your love and commitment.
2. Because she wants to feel a sense of security whether financial, emotional or otherwise.
3. Because she loves your attention and your pursuit of them. She doesn't want to lose the feeling of being wanted and desired.
4. Because you make her feel good and she doesn't want to lose that feeling.
5. Because you make her feel significant by having chosen her.
6. Because she wants to sustain and even grow the experience that she has had up to that point.
7. And yes, she might want to have certainty about having gratifying sex in her life as well.

8. Because she wants to have someone she can always share her feelings with.

9. Because your masculinity enables her to free her femininity and be true to herself.

10. She loves being in love.

11. Because she wants a family; she wants to give birth to life.

12. She wants companionship; a best friend to share her life.

13. She wants your support to chase her dreams and your collaboration to collaborate on dreams together.

14. She wants someone to consistently consume, ravage and take her, and for that to never stop.

The reason these reasons matter is that if the reasons you got married don't consistently manifest themselves after you say "I do", then post-matrimonial pain and frustration become par for the course. Marital upsets happen when our expectations aren't being met and when our needs aren't consistently being met. In other words, when conflict, pain or frustration happen, it's because one or both of you aren't fulfilling what was reasonably implied within your marriage vows. In short, you're not keeping your promises! By now you might be thinking "Yah, but….." Well, just hold your horses and hear me out.

Are You Faithful to Your Mate?

I want to ask you a poignant question. *Have YOU been faithful to your mate?* Because if YOU have, I have to congratulate YOU, as *you* must have an amazing marriage. I'm asking only YOU this question because YOU are the only one that YOU have any direct control or influence over.

Faithfulness has traditionally been associated with sexual fidelity. The question "Have you been faithful to your mate?" immediately conjures up imaginations of temptation, lust and "cheating". However, my question is significantly more encompassing than that. In the context of the implied vows that you made at the altar—have you faithfully loved your mate without condition? Have you faithfully loved your mate without limitation? Have you faithfully offered to them your highest and best self? Have you faithfully fulfilled their sexual needs without prerequisite? Have you faithfully been there for them when they needed your emotional support? Have you faithfully taken care of your physical body and appearance? Have you faithfully forgiven and forgotten wrongdoings? Have you faithfully nurtured your feminine or masculine essence that attracted your mate to you in the first place? Have you faithfully provided for them (in the case of a sole provider) in the way they rightfully expected? Have you faithfully listened to them when they needed to communicate their feelings? Have you faithfully guarded their emotional wellbeing? Have you faithfully supported their dreams and aspirations? If you haven't consistently done these things, what does that imply?

If you're like most people, you might be thinking "F**k, S**t, OMG", or "This is heavy stuff. I've been cheating on my spouse!" Well, hopefully you haven't been *cheating* on your spouse but you might be cheating your spouse and yourself if you aren't actively loving them the way they need, deserve, and rightfully expected at "I do". I know this sounds harsh, but don't take it too hard. Everyone is guilty of this on some level. The big problem arises when you withhold what your mate needs for too long. Whether done intentionally or inadvertently, when a person's needs aren't consistently being met within a relationship, a deficit develops.

Learning to give your mate what they need and loving them fully is a growing experience and that's what marriage is all about—growing your capacity to love, which, as you'll learn, means growing your "self".

Curiously, all human beings have the same inherent needs. Men and women generally have similar if not identical needs, only they typically rank inversely in importance or significance. In other words, what is most important to you may be least important to your mate and vice versa. This is the core element behind God's cosmic joke and the basis for almost all problems, frustrations and misunderstandings in a marriage. They don't call them the opposite sex for nothing. In Section 2 we'll explore how the "opposite" in opposite sex fuels the attraction and desire we want and need to keep your marriage on fire.

At this point, hopefully a huge light bulb is going on in your head. So let's summarize the point of this chapter. If you do nothing but focus on fulfilling your marriage vows and do it with conscious intention, what do you think will happen? What do you think will happen if you daily make the decision to love, honor and cherish your mate? What do you think will happen if you set your "self" aside and act, live and choose your mate like you did on your wedding day? How would things be different if you viewed your mate through the same "eyes" you had when you were courting? What do you think would happen if you discovered how your mate defines love and what makes them feel cherished and significant, and then started doing this? It would have amazing results.

By now you can probably see where the breakdown occurs in a marriage? In the next chapter you'll learn what the 7 core needs are and how filling those needs for your mate will make them love you, want you and adore you like never before. Now we're really having some fun!

ACTION STEPS

1. Reflect on your implicit marriage vows and honestly answer the question "Have I faithfully kept my vows?"
2. Ask yourself why your mate married you in the first place. What I mean is, what needs do they have that they thought you were going to meet for them?
3. Meditate on what it means to be faithful to your mate in the broader sense.
4. Renew your vows to love, honor and cherish, and everything that those words imply.
5. Right now, make a new commitment to yourself, your mate and your relationship. Make a list of what you can you do immediately to make your mate understand they're your number one, your marriage is your priority and you want to take your marriage to new heights. Review your list and choose the 3 things you believe will have the greatest impact and take some form of action to incorporate them into your life NOW.

WHAT MAKES US TICK— THE 7 CORE NEEDS

It goes without saying that men and women are different. In fact, you might think that it's our differences that cause many or most of the problems. It's actually not. It's our lack of understanding, lack of appreciation, and lack of an empowering perspective on these differences that underlie most relationship problems. Here we will talk about understanding our differences, and in a later chapter we will discuss the significance of those differences in more detail.

These differences often reveal themselves in the needs that we have and the manner in which we naturally prefer them to be met. We all adopt or develop rules for what has to happen for us to experience the satisfaction or fulfillment of a need; rules for what has to happen to feel loved, feel secure, feel significant, feel happy, feel healthy, etc. Sometimes the rules we have for experiencing an emotion are too rigid.

For example, if your rules for what has to happen in order for you to feel happy and have a good day require you to get up at 5 AM, go for an hour's run, outperform yesterday's accomplishments, and have mind-blowing sex for 2 hours before sleeping soundly through the night, you're probably not going to be consistently happy. Alternately, if your rule for what has to happen to be happy is simply waking up to the opportunities of another day, you're always going to be happy. Sometimes our rules are so stringent that it's almost impossible for us to get our needs met. Other times they are so silly, it's hard for others to relate to us. Either way, it's critical that we be willing and diligent in learning and recognizing our mate's rules for meeting their needs, whether we can relate to them or not.

A couple of months ago, Kimberly and I had just finished our nightly getting-ready-for-bed ritual. You know, the ever-so-common routine that every couple is familiar with—shower, shave, groom, manicure, spritz, lock door, light candles, start fire, turn back the covers, scatter rose petals, put on some light jazz, climb into bed, ravage each other for an hour and a half, share some wine, cheese and fresh strawberries, re-brush our teeth, climb back into bed, read for 15 minutes, turn out the lights, say "I love you", then go to sleep. Ha! I had you going, didn't I? We don't do that every night, only once or twice a week. On this particular night, the lights went out and I lay there in the dark on my back, with Kimberly's leg routinely draped over my body. She told me she loved me to which I replied "I love you". Well, I don't know if it was the ceiling fan running or the fact that my head was turned slightly away from her but she apparently had not heard my reply. I'm guessing that maybe 5 minutes had gone by and I was drifting into my slumber, when she suddenly said, "Aren't you going to tell me you love me too?" To which I replied, "I did. You must not have heard me". "Oh", she replied "I'm OK now!" She had a need.

At a core level, most problems in a marriage surface when one or more needs are not being met, for one or both people in the relationship.

Later on, we'll explore how these "problems" are actually the most significant opportunities you may ever have for personal growth. In the meantime, while exploring these needs, keep in mind that your mate might articulate their needs in different terms, or may never have communicated them clearly to you. It's common for men and women to assume that the opposite sex has the same needs that they have and that they want those needs met in similar ways.

"At a core level, most problems in a marriage surface when one or more needs are not being met, for one or both people in the relationship."

Even worse, we tend to disregard the hints, requests and petitions of our mate to have their needs filled if what they want doesn't jive with what we want, what we think is important, or how we would want that need met. It just doesn't occur to us that 2 people of the opposite sex or opposite polarities could be so different in the ways we think, process information and communicate. Do you see how convoluted this can be if you don't get this? You see, all humans have the same core needs. They're just rarely ranked in the same order.

Moreover, a woman's and man's needs are almost always in an inverse relationship to each other. In other words, if having sex is a man's way of feeling love and connection, and love and connection is his woman's prerequisite for having sex with him, you can see where the problem occurs. Not only do men and women typically have inversely ranked needs, how those needs are met can be dramatically different. This is one of the facts that makes understanding the opposite sex so challenging.

"...all humans have the same core needs. They're just rarely ranked in the same order."

We think that our partners are just masculine or feminine versions of us, and when they don't act, behave, think or respond like us we think something is wrong with them or our relationship. What's wrong is usually one of 2 things. First, we might be assigning a meaning to the event that is inaccurate, biased or disempowering to the relationship; or second, we are not acting on one of marriage's great opportunities to grow and expand ourselves. In fact, if we are giving any particular instance a disempowering meaning, we are doing that because of our refusal to grow, change or expand ourselves. Change the meaning, change the experience.

Recognize the opportunity to grow and your problem is no longer a problem but rather it's a challenge. Getting better at anything is

"Change the meaning, change the experience."

challenging. If it weren't, it wouldn't be nearly as gratifying to engage in. There is a direct correlation between the level of challenge and personal development something requires, and the level of gratification, enjoyment, and even bliss that one can experience. Look forward to getting into this more, later on.

The differences between men and women can drive you crazy sometimes but they are part of the formula for a passionate marriage. The things that may drive you out of your mind today are actually a part of what attracted you to your mate in the first place. And once you learn to understand and embrace them, they will transform from a source of frustration to a consistent source of comedy, passion and variety.

"One of the secrets to a great marriage is first understanding that your mate is physiologically and biochemically NOT you, and doesn't think like you and then, honoring and embracing this difference."

One of the secrets to a great marriage is first understanding that your mate is physiologically and biochemically NOT you, and doesn't think like you and then, honoring and embracing this difference.

When you do this, you can start meeting their needs, whatever they are, in the way that they need them met; which means when, where and how *they* need them met. Sometimes it may not make any sense to you, but it doesn't matter. You do it because you love them. The exception to this rule is, of course, if your mate's "needs" are destructive. When we get into the 7 core needs, you'll see that there are both healthy and unhealthy ways that we can meet our needs.

When you are ready to lovingly and unselfishly start meeting your mate's needs on a new level, and explore and share your own needs, go to www. GreatMarriageGreatLife.com and click on *Needs Questionnaire* under RE-SOURCES in the menu. We've got a handy questionnaire that will help each of you identify what's missing for you in your relationship. It's an easy way to mutually communicate where you have deficits and the extent of the deficits.

Or, you can start the process of identifying your mate's needs by, well, just asking them. This can actually feel kind of awkward. After all, you should already know this stuff, right? And your mate should know your needs too, yes? Well, strangely enough, most couples find it hard to communicate what we need from our spouse for many reasons that include laziness, insecurity, fear of being judged, fear of being rejected, not being clear ourselves on what we really need, and feeling like our mate should just know on their own without being told.

Marital Sadism

As we explore the 7 core needs and how they relate to your relationship, keep in mind that meeting your mate's needs is a fulfillment of the promises that you made at the altar. It's an act of selfless love and honor. You do it because you love them. Because you want to. You do it without prerequisite, without condition and without expecting anything in return. That's what selfless, un-conditional love is. I know that this might sound like too much to ask, but as you progress through the book, the magic in this will become more evident. If your marriage is rocky, you might be thinking something like, "There's no way I'm going to give the unappreciative, self-righteous, selfish bitch/bastard/ jerk what they need until they clean up their act (i.e., start listening to me, start taking out the trash, give me more sex, romance me, stop yelling, stop arguing, stop complaining, start showing me some respect, start being more affectionate, stop being a slob, start helping around the house, start making more money, etc.).

This is where you need to remember that real love is unconditional. Withholding from your mate in order to manipulate them into giving you what you want or because you don't think they deserve it is nothing short of *marital sadism*. Don't freak out! Sadism is normal in marriage. Everyone does it. No, I'm not talking about the "S" in BDSM. However, now that I think about it, how many married individuals feel like they are in bondage, feel dominated by their mate, or have a masochistic need filled by just staying in a toxic relationship? Far too many, I'm afraid.

In the context of love, the *marital sadism* I'm referring to isn't the kind that happens in dungeons or secret red rooms, but it's equally sick and destructive! However, it's a condition that will diminish over time as we relinquish our ego and grow our capacity to love.

Sadism has been defined as (a) lying to inflict pain, (b) humiliating and demeaning others, (c) restricting the autonomy of someone close to us, (d) withholding from someone, (e) getting someone to comply using intimidation. If most married couples aren't guilty of at least a couple of those things, they're in denial. Here are some examples:

- withholding anything from your mate to cause them pain because they hurt you
- a woman faking an orgasm so her husband will finish up and get it over with
- making your mate pay penance for a wrongdoing
- using your mate's desire for something as leverage to get what you want
- ogling the opposite sex in your spouse's presence
- withholding love or sex to show disapproval of a behavior
- using sex as a bargaining chip to get what you want
- lack of complete honesty and transparency in your relationship.

You might be saying, "What? How is that sadistic?" When you are less than honest about who and what you are; less than honest about what your true intentions are behind your behaviors; less than honest about what your needs are, you are living a lie. And when you live a lie, your relationship is a lie, and you are hurting your mate and yourself. When your marriage lacks the integrity that comes from loving honesty and transparency, what you think you have is but an illusion.

Whatever sense of comfort or security you get out of that isn't real. So let's get real and get on with it by committing to meet our mate's needs at a new level.

> *"When your marriage lacks the integrity that comes from loving honesty and transparency, what you think you have is but an illusion."*

Why Does Infidelity Happen?

As out of context as this question may seem, infidelity is all about human needs. I thought it a good place to set straight something that is largely misunderstood and misrepresented. People commonly think that "cheating" happens for reasons such as:

- men are natural philanders
- women are sluts
- a person is looking to have an affair
- a person is no longer physically attracted to their mate
- a person is sex-deprived
- a person is looking for excitement
- a person got drunk and lost their better judgment
- for vendetta

While these can all be true on some base level, the underlying reason that almost all extra-marital sex happens is because a deep emotional need, or needs are consistently NOT being filled within the relationship or in one's life. When someone (a friend, acquaintance or co-worker) comes along and fills that missing need at a significant level, a strong emotional attachment develops, a positive association with that person is formed, and a magnetism grows. More often than not, affairs are more about meeting unfulfilled needs for significance, unconditional love and acceptance than they are about sex. "Infidelity" and its accompanying fall-out as we are accustomed to seeing it, is often just a symptom of the real unfaithfulness going on in the relationship. The person being blamed or accused of being the "cheater!" by the "victim" is often just a smokescreen for the "victim's" own unfaithfulness to the vows they took. Don't freak out and throw the book in the trash. I know this is hard to take but we are all guilty on some level! I'm just calling it like it is.

In all fairness, there is another notable reason infidelity happens and that is the need to feel alive. After 2 decades or more of raising kids and being committed to your job and family, people often tire of the predictability and monotony of their life. It may have been good but it was the "same" good for too long.

You can tire of the best restaurant in town if that's the only place you ever eat. Correction: You can tire of the restaurant if they never change the menu up or offer interesting and unexpected specials. A really great restaurant does 2 things. First, they provide you with a predictable, high level of quality service and food. Second, and most importantly, their menu isn't a foregone conclusion. They are careful to keep your favorites on the menu while spicing things up with nightly specials, seasonal menu changeovers and even occasional remodels. They further enhance your experience with varying entertainment and personalized service. This is the formula to keep customers coming back for more.

The good news is, when you are faithful to your mate in terms of consistently meeting their needs at a high level, including their need for variety and uncertainty, the question of sexual infidelity is completely off the table.

"...when you are faithful to your mate in terms of consistently meeting their needs at a high level, including their need for variety and uncertainty, the question of sexual infidelity is completely off the table."

I mean, it doesn't even enter into the picture. However, meeting your mate's needs at a high level requires consistent personal growth, and that's what marriage is all about—growing, expanding, stretching and deepening. Without engaging in this process, we would remain emotional and spiritual 12-year-olds (no offense to 12-year-olds) and never fully experience the richness of growing up into our fullness.

Another Way of Looking At It

When you have a history of pain and frustration in your relationship, it's often challenging to bridge the gap between what you know you should do, and what you will do. This is why your marriage "problems" don't go away. Problems occur when we have the opportunity to make a difference by growing ourselves in some way, but we resist the opportunity.

Many times we resist making a change because it feels difficult, overwhelming or maybe we're not sure where to begin. I encourage you to focus on taking the first step, however small it may be. A journey of a thousand miles begins with just one step. When you commit to a small change in the right direction and are consistent, you will experience a big change over time.

Our habits are deeply grooved in our mind from repetition, making it difficult to change our knee-jerk responses and reactions. I've found the best way for me to initiate change, is by contemplating how I will choose to respond next time in a similar situation, and then allowing time to thoughtfully respond before my typical reaction.

If it's a new endeavor I seek, I make the phone call, take the class, and marshal resources that get me on track to accomplishing my goal.

We resist or ignore the prompting for any one of many reasons including, but not limited to, our reluctance to make ourselves vulnerable; our reluctance to let go of our ego; our reluctance to take responsibility for the situation; fear of change; fear of loss of love; fear of discomfort; fear of facing the truth, and even fear of exposure. The funny thing is that all these

"Problems occur when we have the opportunity to make a difference by growing ourselves in some way, but we resist the opportunity."

emotional responses are signals for you to face your rough edges, grow up and start uncovering the real you, which is pure love. Loving your mate with pure, unconditional, unlimited and unrequited love requires you to discover and embrace your true potential as a human being.

And guess what, when you do that, they will become your biggest, raving fan and cheering squad all wrapped into one.

It's interesting to me that we're all familiar with the concept of meeting the needs of others without asking anything in return. It's a common practice in the business world. The highest performers and best networkers in any field

"Loving your mate with pure, unconditional, unlimited and unrequited love requires you to discover and embrace your true potential as a human being."

know what it means to help others achieve their goals in order to achieve their own. If you are at the top of your game and you want to grow your sales, your audience, your fan base or your referral network, what do you do? You give,

give, and give without asking anything in return. In other words, you help others get what they want and exceed their expectations in the process. By helping others meet their needs, you create raving fans who will enthusiastically reciprocate by helping you get what you want. On a base level, this is what marriage is all about.

So how do you apply this to your mate? Well, as you read the rest of this chapter, ask yourself: How can I meet these needs for my lover? What have I been missing? Once again, the obvious thing to do is ask.

Questions like "What can I do to make you feel more loved?" or "What, if anything, do you feel is missing in our marriage? I really want to know because you mean the world to me, and I want you to be happy." A more subtle (and genius) but more time-consuming way to identify which of your lover's needs might be deficient is to start taking your affection, listening skills, focus and romance up a notch or two and seeing how they respond. If you are sensitive to their responses, you can often deduce what their deficits might be. However, what you deduce on your own may be, at best, only partially accurate and, oftentimes, completely off base. There is no substitute for just asking what you can do to be a better husband, wife and lover. Thinking you can figure your mate out completely on your own without insider information from them is foolishness. Sometimes we just need to be thrown a bone.

Often, when you learn what your lover's needs are, the importance they place on them might not make any sense to you. It doesn't matter. Just lovingly and honorably embrace them, and get to work being the woman or man that they deserve. Don't forget this is all about meeting the needs of your partner. You can't control your partner. You can't change your partner. You can't tell your partner what to do. However, what you can do is inspire them. You can give them a whole new set of behaviors to respond to. You can create an environment that nurtures love, honor, passion and respect. And I'm telling you, if you have love, honor, passion and respect, you have the makings of a really *hot* and *passionate* affair with your mate.

So, if you can playfully communicate with your partner, then just wade in and start doing your research. If you feel less comfortable articulating your deeper needs to your mate, filling out the downloadable *Needs Questionnaire* on our website is a great place to start. If that seems daunting, we have private facilitation and coaching available on a limited basis.

Caveat

This is where I need to give you a caveat. If there are emotional or physical needs that have consistently gone unmet within your relationship, there is on some level an absence of quality communication, loving behavior and honor. If you have needs that have gone unmet in your relationship, chances are that past attempts to communicate your needs have been met with less than favorable reactions. Or maybe your mate's attempts to communicate their needs have fallen on deaf ears, or even worse, met with resistance. If either is the case, before sharing your *Needs Questionnaires* with each other, it's important that you both be in a mutual state of commitment to your relationship and mutually agree to ground rules that will help mitigate any negative reactions.

The purpose of the sharing is to *share*—share without defense, without judgment, and without argument. Remember, the purpose of meeting your mate's needs isn't really about you. It's mostly about them. The part of it that *is* about you is the part of you that may need to grow in order for you to meet their needs. I never said this would be painless.

In intimate relationships, our mates often lose touch with their authentic selves and vice versa, because when we've expressed ourselves or our needs to each other, we've met each other with judgment, ridicule, censure or disapproval. When this happens, in order to get the love, attention, or acceptance that we need, we often start masquerading who we really are to reduce conflict and increase acceptance. When we do this, we lose the ability to experience intimacy and have fulfillment within the relationship at a deep level.

So, if you are committed to yourself, your mate and your relationship, commit right now to meeting their needs in whatever way they need instead of what you think they need, as long as they are not destructive. Choose right now to honor and respect your mate's preferences, and also to give them the space to authentically express their needs without judgment and censure. You don't have to like your eggs the same or have the same music preferences to have a deeply intimate relationship. You do, however, need to have a deep level of honor and respect for your mate and yourself.

If your mate has a desire or need that makes you feel uncomfortable, share your feelings lovingly but at the same time make an effort to move in their direction. If their desires go against your rules; you need to collaborate together to find a middle ground you're both happy and satisfied with.

Before I get into the 7 core needs, I want to give credit to 3 forerunners in the fields of psychology, personal development and family counseling who have brought the significance of human needs and their integral roles in our relationships to the forefront. These extraordinary educators are Dr. Willard F. Harley, Jr., Cloé Madanes and Anthony Robbins.

The 7 Core Needs

Core Need #1: Certainty

We all need to have certainty in our lives. Certainty comes from many sources that are equally important, namely security, love and health. Certainty is knowing that no matter what, your partner will be there for you and that you are unconditionally loved, cherished and adored.

Certainty comes from a belief in your resourcefulness, knowing that no matter what happens, together with your partner you can pull through anything. Certainty might mean not having to worry about putting food on the table or a roof over your head. It's knowing that the meeting of your physical needs is not in question. Certainty means not having to worry about the unknown. It enables you to sleep at night. Certainty also comes from believing in a higher power.

Gentlemen: A woman feels certainty or security when she has no financial pressure. Don't ever allow her to be in a position where she feels financially insecure. For one, she deserves a life of certainty and comfort where she can be free to allow her femininity to flow. And two, uncertainty (any kind of uncertainty) can diminish her desire for sex. When a woman feels honored and adored, she feels certain of her man's fidelity. When a woman's core values (namely security, love, and wellbeing) are not being met, it is difficult for her to want to fill secondary values such as sexual connection and expression.

Women's brains are wired like a bowl of spaghetti where everything is connected to everything. If she's stressed about money, the kids or some imminent threat, it's almost impossible for her to have gratifying sex with you.

Years ago while on a walk in the forest engaged in a dynamic conversation, we made the revolutionary distinction that sex was a great barometer for decision making. In short, if in pursuing a goal we would experience more stress, uncertainty or threaten some other core value that would lead to less sex, it was the wrong decision.

Ladies: A man may equally experience certainty in his strength (health), his ability to provide for his family, his belief in a higher power, and in your commitment to him. As revolutionary as this may seem, a guy finds certainty in having sex with his wife whereas a woman generally wants certainty before having sex with her husband. For a guy, sex is a way of reconnection and reassurance that "everything is cool between us." It's also a good reset button for us at the end of a stressful day.

What provides each of us certainty may differ due to differences in gender and core values. Never assume that your partner's needs are the same as yours, or that their needs are met just because yours are met. You must walk in the direction of your partner with a spirit of reciprocity. Just because a guy doesn't feel like talking doesn't mean he shouldn't fill his woman's need to talk, and do it lovingly. He will soon discover the reward in knowing and understanding his wife more intimately, and will more willingly engage as time goes by. Likewise, just because a woman doesn't desire sex doesn't mean it's not at that moment an essential component to the health and wellbeing of their marriage, and her husband's sanity. Curiously enough, the stereotypical roles described above can just as well be reversed.

Core Need #2: Uncertainty/Variety

In spite of our need for concrete certainty, life would be pretty boring without variety, surprise, and unexpected challenge, hence our need for uncertainty. Too much uncertainty, however, breeds insecurity so there is a delicate balance to be maintained.

Gentlemen: For women, constructive uncertainty comes with never knowing what their lover may surprise them with next—a dozen roses, a romantic picnic under the stars, or perhaps an afternoon at the spa.

Ladies: For men, it happens naturally just being with a woman, if she lives authentically. A woman who has embraced her femininity and is given the space, freedom and certainty to be true to her essence will give a man all the uncertainty he craves. A woman's natural hormonal shifts, ever-changing emotions, and the dramatic unfolding of her mystery can be a fulfilling source of variety in a man's life.

Uncertainty also comes from taking on new challenges or learning new skills. It comes from journeying into new territory not always completely prepared. It's taking a road trip without any reservations; it's trying new ethnic cuisine; it's adding a dash of spice to your life; it's taking your sexual experience to new levels; it's surprising each other! Never allow the fun and romance to become too predictable. Predictability breeds certainty, and too much certainty extinguishes the flame of desire.

Incidentally, it is certainty that makes a marriage good, but it is uncertainty that makes it passionate. Learning to navigate a path between certainty and uncertainty is at the core of experiencing a life-long love affair.

It's important to not treat your mate like a "girlfriend", telling them every detail of your life and day, just as when you were courting there was continual surprise and things left unsaid. Give yourself room to be a little bit of a mystery, and not an open book. This is not to intentionally hide important information but to give them room to discover elements about you on their own.

Core Need #3: Significance

We all need to feel significant, that we are important to someone, and that our existence has meaning. We naturally seek ways to validate our uniqueness. We find significance in our careers, college degrees, achievements, societal roles, athletic prowess, size, strength, religious affiliations, the way we dress, and the clubs we belong to. We get significance in being a parent and a lover or provider. Some people meet this need through destructive means like alcohol, drugs and criminal behavior. If you think about it, a car thief feels pretty significant while racing down the road in a stolen car with 3 squad cars after him.

Within our marriage, we have a deep need to be significant to our spouse. That significance comes from consistent validation that we are the one they have chosen. We desire and need to know that we are appreciated—not once in a while but all the time. Everyone wants to know they matter and are not taken for granted.

Your mate demonstrates what makes them feel significant by their actions, whether it's working overtime to provide for their family, running a household, creating memorable experiences for the family... Notice how they spend their time and recognize them for the efforts they make to improve the quality of your lives.

For example, I spend a lot of my time cooking because I believe that healthy food is a major contributor to how we feel, and our quality of life in the present and the future. Because I invest so much of my time towards this effort, it's extremely meaningful to me when my family takes notice and shows appreciation.

Gentlemen: She really wants to know that she's appreciated and that the second income she brings home (if this is the case) is a killer contribution. Yeah, I know you appreciate her, but she needs to know it daily. She needs to know that you appreciate her sharing her life with you. She needs appreciation for all the little things she does that make life easier for you. She needs appreciation for just being a woman. I personally have the highest reverence for women and exalt them above all else on earth. If she's a mother, she is by default one seriously significant human being. Let her know it.

Ladies: A man gains much of his significance in life through providing for and pleasing his woman. Trust me on this. We feel like heroes every time we provide you any kind of pleasure, comfort or solution to a problem. When you are happy, we feel like conquerors. If we buy a house you love, we feel significant. If we take you to a movie that you really enjoy, we feel responsible. If we take you out to dinner and you rave about how good it was, we feel like we cooked the meal ourselves. When you experience an orgasm, we feel extremely validated. If you are multi-orgasmic, well, then we feel like gods.

Ladies, men need significance 20 times more then we think they do and if they act like they don't need it, it's 50 times more.

Core Need #4: Love/Connection

Is love all you need? The answer is YES! And NO! No, in the sense that love is just one of the 7 core needs. But yes, in that if you love in the most complete sense of the word, your love will translate into the fulfillment of all 7 core needs. Most people in long-term relationships say they love their spouse, but they don't really *love* their spouse. Learning to love deeply and broadly is what marriage is all about. Mastery of love is not a destination but a journey, and marriage is the vehicle that takes you on that journey. So buckle up.

Caution: Don't bail on me now with all the love talk. Trust me, this is just starting to get good.

What Love Is

The ancient Greeks identified 3 types of love. Each is really important to understand in its relationship to marriage and sex: agape, philos and eros.

Agape Love is God-like love; it's unconditional and stretches across all humanity. It has no boundary and is in a spiritual sense, divine. It's the love you have for mankind; the love that sends your heart out to starving children in Ethiopia.

Philos Love is friendship love. It's the meat and potatoes of a relationship. It fosters reciprocity, a give-and-take in the meeting of each other's needs. Philos is experienced between good friends, siblings and spouses.

Eros Love is erotic love. It is the need for and expression of sexual desire, affection and physical intimacy. Eros is the experience of falling in love. It's the feeling of euphoria when you are physically and emotionally attracted to your lover. It is romantic love.

What makes marriage so unique is that it is the only human relationship that encompasses all 3 kinds of love simultaneously. This is a powerful realization—and the reason why I believe that a great marriage is the pinnacle of human experience.

Love is knowing your partner, for in knowledge there is strength. Couples who have an intimate knowledge of each other are better equipped to prevent and weather conflict and marital storms. What does it mean to know your partner? It means to be in touch. It means to always know what their desires, hopes and dreams are. It means to know their beliefs, fears and inhibitions. It comes from communicating about everything that is going on in each other's lives. It's knowing what makes them feel loved. How can you know someone if you don't know their rules for experiencing love?

Love is knowing what makes your partner tick, what juices them, what their passions are—and knowing the most current versions of these things. Love is communicating your needs to one another. It's knowing what her/his favorite flower, song, food, movie and book is. Love is keeping the house stocked with your lover's favorite snack. Love is taking her dancing when I hate (I mean, "prefer not to" sweetie) to dance. Love is not forcing your preferences down each other's throats. Love is honoring and embracing your differences. Love is never minding how long she takes to "get ready" to go any-where. Love is stretching yourself to meet your mate's needs on their terms. It's sharing the trivial as well as the significant.

To be intimate is to share the intimate - your deepest desires, dreams and expe-riences with your mate. It doesn't mean dumping the minutia of everyday life. I encourage you to elevate your conversation to one that is gratifying and beneficial to you both.

Oftentimes when individuals look outside their marriage to have their needs for love met, it's because they've begun to live separate lives resulting from lack of knowledge of each other. We all remember "The Piña Colada Song" by Rupert Holmes. It poignantly exemplifies how often we look "out-side" for what we already have near us. The song tells of a man who, bored with his relationship, looks in the personal ads for new possibilities. He finds an intriguing ad written by a seemingly very sensual woman looking for someone who likes Piña Coladas, getting caught in the rain, and making love on the beach. He responds to the ad and suggests meeting in a bar. Later, he waits in the bar for her only to see his "own lovely lady" walk in. He tells her that "he never knew" she likes Piña Coladas, etc., and that she was the lady he'd looked for. "Come with me and escape."

Human Need #5: Autonomy

As much as we need love and connection with other human beings, to really benefit from that love and connection, we need a sense of autonomy and independence. By autonomy and independence, I really mean a distinct sense of self. Just like our opposing needs for certainty and uncertainty need to be met in order to feel both safe and alive, we need to have a healthy sense of individuality to be able to truly love and connect with another.

This healthy sense of self is called *differentiation*, a subject that we'll explore more in a later chapter. In the context of marriage, autonomy is when 2 uniquely differentiated (separate and different) people choose to be together and support each other in the meeting of their needs. Autonomy is growing your own unique sense of *You* while simultaneously integrating *You* with your mate. You do this in love and by choice rather than by sacrifice or abdication. The yin/yang symbol illustrates how this works. It exemplifies how 2 distinct but complementary and polarizing energies dovetail to form a complete whole. Neither gives up its essence, but rather shares its essence with the other with profound, alchemical effect.

In my first book, *Winning at the Game of Wife*, I shared the story of the Dame Ragnelle from Geoffrey Chaucer's, *The Canterbury Tales*. In a quest to save his king from certain death, the noble knight, Sir Gawain, must discover and deliver to his king the answer to a most confounding question, "What is it that a woman desires most?" The most loyal knight, finds himself in a quandary when the answer is offered to him in exchange for marrying an old, hideous hag. However, his loyalty pays off when, by giving his new bride what she truly desired, he is rewarded with not just the answer to his profound question, but also by her transformation into a raving beauty. What he learned that a woman desired most was, *autonomy*—the desire to be authentically herself and choose for herself.

Core Need #6: Growth

Marriage is the ultimate opportunity for growth. And growth equals expansion. Expansion means living more, loving more, and everything that implies. It implies that you expand emotionally, mentally, physically, financially, spiritually and sexually. Someone once said that you're either growing or dying. Think about it; nothing but simple life forms can live long in a stagnant pond. It's dead, devoid of life.

Growth is a fundamental human need because it is the process of moving forward to self-realization and knowing God, whatever God means to you. Growth is what makes you feel alive.

Interestingly enough, growth does not come naturally to many people, and marriage offers you the biggest opportunity for it. Problems in a relationship are a blessing in disguise. They are completely natural and to be expected; a signal that something needs to change, that it's time to grow. If you have a health problem, you tackle it head-on and make radical changes in your lifestyle. A health problem is a wake-up call that you have been doing one or many cumulative things wrong. If you have a problem in your business, you tackle it, learn from it, make whatever changes are required, and grow the business to the next level. In business, whenever you have a problem you don't say, "That's just the way I am."

When you have a problem in other areas of your life and don't take a course of action to remedy it, you reap the consequences— businesses can fail, your house may be foreclosed on, or your kid will get expelled. We must take care of problems while they are small.

If you think about it, no one can really be happy doing the same thing at the same level for very long. You will either get bored and frustrated or you will push yourself to new levels that keep you challenged. We grow by learning new skills and languages, by taking on new challenges, by stretching outside our comfort zone. We grow by entertaining new paradigms, by considering the needs of others before our own. Growth always provides perspective because you can only appreciate where you are, by looking back at where you've come from.

Contributing to an environment that allows your partner to grow is a mature act of love, and an impetus for your own development. Examples of this might be providing for and supporting them in:

- their personal interests
- their spiritual exploration and development
- tennis lessons
- art classes
- foreign language classes
- specialty cooking classes
- starting a new business
- a spiritual retreat
- a couples' tantric sex retreat
- a personal development seminar
- reading a book together on *Cracking the Code to Marital Bliss*
- learning to ride a motorcycle or fly an airplane
- taking her to dance lessons

How fun does this sound!!! I love pursuing new hobbies as a surprise to my lover. Gaining proficiency at a new skill is one avenue I use to continuously make me an unfolding mystery that keeps him guessing.

Growth is, well...Growing Up!

Growth is also a huge part of maintaining the polarity and consequently the dynamic of desire in a marriage. When your partner is growing, learning, changing and evolving, it keeps you on your toes. It helps you maintain a sense of wonder, interest and curiosity in them. Growth helps support the differentiation between 2 people that is necessary for sensual desire. Personal growth is expanding our capacity to love.

What do you want your marriage to look like in 5, 10, 15 years? When you're grow-ing, the love and passion will magnify over time. How cool is that!!!

Core Need #7: Contribution

Contribution is your way of giving back, of making a difference. It's your participation in making the world a better place. It's not uncommon for people to struggle with having a sense of purpose in their lives. "Why am I here?" or "What's the point of my life?" are questions that eventually come up once the noise and glitz of modern life start to fade in significance. We need to feel that our lives "have meaning" as Viktor Frankl put it in his monumental book, *Man's Search for Meaning.* The answer to the "meaning" question is almost always found in tandem with the answer to the "contribution" question, and in the filling of our need for significance.

Every person has a unique talent, gift or insight. Our unique gift might be our intense passion for something that people aren't normally passionate about. It might be cooking, tennis, gardening, mechanical engineering, teaching, voice, guitar, sculpting, medicine, massage, writing, hairstyling, shrub trimming, inventing, speaking, or the gift of prophecy. Whatever your gift, talent or passion, the one thing you need to appreciate most is that we each have a unique way of expressing that gift, talent or passion. We each have a unique "voice." That's why every art form in the world never runs out of individuals to express its interpretations. Every painter, singer, sculptor, composer, graphic designer, cake decorator and jeweler is unique. Likewise, every physician, dentist, engineer, carpenter, teacher, mother and yoga instructor is unique. We may not be in a unique line of work, but we certainly have a unique way of communicating our work and expressing it to the world.

So how can we each best serve our fellow man and contribute most sig-nificantly? This is my answer to the question. In your marriage, support each other's need to contribute whether that means putting 20 bucks in the plate at church, donating to a local charity, or being an outstanding parent. Your greatest contribution might come in raising children in a non-dysfunctional environment. I can't think of one more significant or honorable. Maybe your contribution is being the best husband or wife you can be to set a higher standard for friends and family. I am certain the biggest contribution you can make to society at large is in your own home.

Nevertheless, I think that life's true purpose is to be true to yourself.

"I think that life's true purpose is to be true to yourself."

When you dig deep and find that *thing* that stirs your passion and lifts you to a higher place—that love for something that must be shared in a way only you can share—you'll find that part of yourself. Being true to yourself is living your "personal legend" as Paulo Coelho puts it in his book *The Alchemist*. It's living your passion and expressing it in the way that only *you* can, using your unique "voice." And in the process, your scent, your flavor, your essence will linger and the world will be a better place because of you.

ACTION STEPS

1. Identify your mate's needs that are not being met on their terms and start meeting them. This may require you to ask them what you can do to make them feel more loved, honored, appreciated or respected. If you just watch and listen, I think you'll know what they are without asking.

2. Contemplate whether or not you have needs that are being met in a way that is destructive to your personal health and wellbeing, and that of your relationship. Then look for healthy alternatives that you could replace these behaviors with.

3. Ask yourself how you can meet your mate's needs for certainty, uncertainty, love, significance, autonomy, personal growth and contribution on a higher level. To do this, you've got to stop looking to them to have your needs met and focus on meeting theirs. That's what love is all about.

LOVE IS THE
ULTIMATE FREEDOM

I WOULD BE REMISS not to include the following Bible text in a discussion on love. This is not a religious view, rather it describes what love is, I believe, in terms of agape and philos. I encourage you to read it slowly and thoughtfully.

> *Love is patient, love is kind. It does not envy, it does not boast, it is not proud. It does not dishonor others, it is not self-seeking, it is not easily angered, it keeps no record of wrongs. Love does not delight in evil but rejoices with the truth. It always protects, always trusts, always hopes, always perseveres.*
>
> —1 Corinthians 13:4-7 NIV

Well, I think that about says it all. And since most of Western civilization is Christian, and most Christians have read or heard this very notable text, we should be a "nation of love" and love must be permeating our marriages and families, right? Wrong!

But why? Because most people are hypocrites. They're Sunday morning (part-time) Christians. I would love to go on an extensive rant about this, but it would digress too far from our subject. That said, it is difficult to separate a discussion on love from spirituality, and spirituality from religion. Which brings me to a side note. Many have asked me why there seems to be so much marital dissatisfaction and even divorce within the "love" communities of Christianity, Buddhism, child education, philanthropy and healthcare. After all, most people involved in these spiritual modalities and pursuits have a love mindset in some way, shape or form. They love god, love humanity, love their kids, and love the earth. What's going on?

Here's my answer: People "love" to the level of their personal growth.

"People "love" to the level of their personal growth."

In other words, we love in whatever capacity and to whatever extent is easy and comfortable for us. We put all our energy into that and ignore the other attributes of love that make us uncomfortable and might cause us some personal reckoning and growth. That's why a dedicated church pastor might be 100% committed to his congregation while simultaneously enduring a sexless, dispassionate marriage at home. Or for instance, take a mother who might donate all her free time to a homeless shelter but have an alienated 15-year-old kid who feels insignificant and invisible. These are examples of people who love in ways that are comfortable and yet forsake love where it may require them to stretch, expand and grow in their own divinity.

The truth is, if we all truly loved, we would all have happy, meaningful, rewarding and passionate marriages. If we have less than that, it is because we have yet to develop our capacity to love in all its facets and do it without limitation or condition. Your marriage is the only place you can develop this capacity. Marriage compels you, requires you and inspires you to grow in love or it just doesn't work. More accurately, it doesn't grow to its intended place. To give up on marriage is to give up on yourself and your greatest opportunity to grow as a human being.

> *"To give up on marriage is to give up on yourself and your greatest opportunity to grow as a human being."*

Some of you might throw the book (the "good book" that is) at me for saying this but *you don't learn to love in church,* or any other spiritual modality for that matter. You learn *about* love. You learn about love conceptually. Developing the capacity to love happens in tandem with personal and spiritual growth, neither of which seem to parallel church attendance. There is arguably no environment that fosters personal and spiritual growth more than marriage when its true potential is fully embraced. That's why I hypothesize that the path of marriage and the path to godliness parallel each other. Or perhaps more rightly, they are one and the same.

To progress along this path requires 100% of your commitment. Most people think that marriage is a 50/50 proposition. The problem with this view is that it disempowers you from making any meaningful change in your relationship. If you're always waiting for your mate to step up to the plate, make the first gesture, or do something deserving of your love, you're going to go nowhere fast. Marriage is a 100/100 proposition. This means that you've got to take 100% responsibility for your relationship. You've got to commit yourself to meeting your mate's needs at a higher level with no expectations. That's true love. When you expect something in return, the act of love loses its purity. Giving and acting in love in and of itself is to experience love at a deep level.

So now that you've recommitted to yourself to grow in love and recommitted to love your mate in an ever-greater capacity, let's explore this thing called love a little more.

Unconditional Love

Is love the answer to growing? Actually, unconditional love is the answer. However, just writing "unconditional love" feels wrong. It's like writing the words "animal meat". I think it's safe to assume that when someone says they like to eat meat they are referring to animal meat as opposed to coconut meat or soy meat. Meat is meat. By the same token, love is love. If it's conditional then it's not really love, is it? It's actually something other than love. If not love, then what?

Even recognizing and acknowledging that we demonstrate "conditional" love to our loved ones isn't enough if we fail to take ownership of the fact that we often exhibit behaviors that are anything but love. Learning to love "unconditionally" *is* learning to love. I want to propose that learning to love without conditions is the process of growing up, and realizing our highest and best self. It is, as put in I Corinthians 13, the process of putting away childish things.

Learning to love without condition is a prerequisite to a passionate life-long love affair. It's even a prerequisite to a "good" marriage. Notice the italics on the word learning. Learning to love is a life-long process. That's why you don't want to give up on school (marriage) until you've learned the lessons (gifts) it has for you. Once you've learned the lessons (developing your capacity to love), you get to graduate to the next grade, not quit school.

Marriage isn't about shacking up, although that's part of it.

Marriage isn't about ensuring a good sex life. Many can testify to that.

Marriage isn't about having kids, although that's part of it too.

It's not even so much about providing security anymore.

Marriage is about spiritual growth and expanding your capacity to love. The message in most spiritual practices is one of love. The goal of most spiritual practitioners is to experience, grow in, and become that love. This is often described as salvation, union with God, liberation, nirvana or bliss. What these things really describe is the state in which we are living in love, free from the constraints of all the trappings of our ego.

Forgiving Love

I don't know how many times I read the words from 1 Corinthians 13, quoted earlier, before I noticed an interesting omission. It doesn't say *"love is forgiving"* anywhere. How could Paul have missed that? We all know that forgiveness is next to godliness, right? Oh sorry, it's been said that cleanliness is next to godliness. Anyway, if you really have unconditional love for someone, you forgive them for their wrongs, right? Forgiveness is something that people ask me about all the time. "How do I forgive him/her for what they did?" "How do I forgive him/her for cheating on me, for abandoning me, for neglecting me, for hurting me?"

This is where we miss the point of forgiveness. Forgiveness isn't a gift to bestow on someone else. It's not a power we have to absolve someone of their sins against us. Who do we think we are anyway—God? We often use forgiveness as a tool to gain leverage over someone that hurt us. We withhold it until they've done their time, suffered enough, or have atoned for their sins.

Forgiveness isn't something we do for other people, it's something we do for ourselves to cleanse our own hearts and minds of thoughts, feelings and meanings that cause us pain. How do I know this? Let's go back to I Corinthians 13. If you read it carefully one more time, you'll notice it says that "[love] keeps no record of wrongs." In other words, if love keeps no record of wrongs, then there is never anything to forgive!

In love, there is never anything to forgive. Love frees you from the past. Love frees you from guilt. Love is the only place where you can realize your highest and best self. Keeping an account of what your mate has done to upset, offend or hurt you does not serve you. It does not inspire you to be the best you that you can be. You cannot move forward when you chain yourself to the past. We all make mistakes, get over it! If you can't forget, you can certainly change the meanings that you've given to things. We touched on this in our discussion of the 3 components of achieving a quality state. If you're going to assign a meaning to something, you might as well give it a meaning that serves and empowers you to be your highest self, and go forward in love.

It's easy to keep score, anyone can do that, but it's much more empowering to let go of bad memories and mistakes that you and your mate made. Painful experiences can make an indelible mark in our minds, especially when coupled with strong emotion. I think of bad memories as a bad movie. How many of us would intentionally watch the same horrible movie over and over again? It doesn't serve you but instead binds you to the past, wasting the precious time of the present. When an old memory creeps up, nip it in the bud. Don't indulge yourself and relive it. It will contaminate the moment and nothing good will come of it. Instead redirect your thoughts to love, and how you can do your part to grow and best serve your relationship.

The Freedom in Real Love

People make mistakes, break rules, violate codes, and cross over lines. We all do it and we do it all the time, at least in small ways. True love is offering your mate an environment where they are free to be authentic and make mistakes without fear of being judged, rejected, or condescended to. That's what we give our children. We let them know that no matter what, we will be there for them. We give them the space to grow and discover.

So why is it that so many men feel their relationship is a ball and chain, where they can't be authentic and have room to be themselves? Ladies, in an effort to maintain our sense of certainty, we often create boundaries in our relationship that constrain our mate to a limited playing field that restricts them from being able to fulfill their needs. For example, you may pressure them to give up inherently risky activities that fill their masculine need for a sense of freedom. It's important that we don't smother our spouse. We need to support their aspirations, and help them achieve whatever it is that makes them tick, drives them forward, and makes them excited to get up in the morning.

However, we do that within the confines of set parameters. Studies have shown that if you take away the security fence surrounding an elementary school, children feel vulnerable and will congregate in the center of the schoolyard out of fear. However, when a boundary fence is in place, the children will venture out to the very edges of it. They enjoy a greater sense of freedom when they are free to play within constraints.

It's the same way in marriage. A marriage relationship done right provides the best of both worlds. It gives us the certainty of being loved and accepted unconditionally while simultaneously allowing us to be authentic

"True love is offering your mate an environment where they are free to be authentic... We give them the space to grow and discover"

and true to ourselves. I'm not talking about having an "open" marriage. I'm talking about creating an environment where we are inspired by love rather than constrained by the fear of loss, judgment or rejection. We construct the figurative fence around our marriage because its existence makes the game of marriage more rewarding.

Everything in life that provides any deep sense of fulfillment has rules. Soccer wouldn't be nearly as fun if there were no rules or boundaries. A player could just run with the ball in any direction they wanted and do anything they wanted with the ball. It would be like the soccer version of Mad Max. However, when you play within the boundaries of the field and by a given set of rules, then you have a game. The level of fulfillment you experience will then be directly proportionate to your level of focus, level of skill development, and fitness.

In the context of your marriage, establishing rules and boundaries is a necessary prerequisite to engaging in the game. The rules give you the opportunity to discover and manifest your highest and best self. The question is, how can you increase your focus, your skill level and your fitness? How much love can you bring to your relationship? How much adventure, excitement and variety can you bring? How special can you make your mate feel? What amazing things might come out of loving at a new level with less judgment, censure and withholding?

As with the game of tennis, the boundaries in a marriage are virtual. You're not playing inside a cage. You don't have to stay within the boundaries or play by the rules. You do that by choice. You choose, moment by moment, to honor the boundaries and the rules. That's your freedom. You are also free to increase the challenge and therefore the potential for fulfillment by holding yourself to a higher standard, increasing your skill, tightening up your game, and taking your fitness to a new level. The "good book" suggests that there is freedom in obedience. Without the constraints of the boundaries and rules, we would never have the impetus to grow. There would be no point. So it is, in your marriage.

If you are one of those who rebel against being held to the standards and limitations of arbitrary rules, I have an answer for you in the form of a story. Besides being a medical doctor, my grandfather was an extraordinary contributor as a researcher, educator and mentor. He lived his life to a high standard of excellence. He often collaborated with "establishment" but at the same time never really trusted it. One day he divulged to me that when he was in college, he despised being accountable to the rules imposed upon him. He rebelled against the academic standards and curfews that restricted his personal freedoms and pressured his performance. So what did he do? He decided that he wasn't going to follow any of the school's rules. Instead, he would set stricter rules and higher performance standards for himself so that the school's rules wouldn't apply to him. He was no longer accountable to the schools administration but instead to himself. He was the ruler of his own universe, master of his own destiny. Setting higher standards for himself ironically freed him from the limitations of the institution that was educating him and also freed him to focus on what was most important to him.

Choosing Love

The study of human psychology has shown us that when given too many choices, we generally lose the capacity for contentment. In his book *Flow*, Mihaly Csikszentmihalyi stated, "But the inevitable consequence of equally attractive choices is uncertainty of purpose". Narrowing the playing field or reducing our options forces us to focus more psychic energy into one place and when our focus is concentrated, our capacity for enjoyment and richness is greater. Mihaly then goes on to say, "If the rules of a game become too flexible, …it is difficult to attain a flow experience." In other words, when we open ourselves up to too many options, our focus is often diluted and we become subject to confusion and discontent.

If you've ever gone to a restaurant with a 7-page menu you know what I'm talking about. When there is too much to choose from, you end up struggling with your choice and then second-guessing it after you've made it. I prefer restaurants that have a 1-page menu made up of one red meat dish, one chicken dish, one fish dish, one vegetarian dish, and maybe one gluten-free dish. It's quick and easy to order. If you are a vegetarian, there's no second-guessing what to order. It's the same in your marriage. If you are a dedicated one-woman man or one-man woman, you stop looking around at your options and start focusing your psychic energy into the one who matters most. In other words, you start really loving the one you're with and forget about the rest.

There's an old country song that says, "Dance with the one that brought you and you can't go wrong." Choosing to dance with the one you are with and stop looking around the room for another option does 3 things for you. It gets you focused, it keeps you present, and it gets you out of your head and into your heart. Monogamy isn't so much about the limitations associated with making a commitment to one's partner, it's more about the freedom associated with making a commitment to one's self. It's about integrity and setting high standards for one's self.

Whatever we focus on we make significant, important, and enjoy at a higher level. What would happen if we focused on our marriage as if it was more important than friends, extended family, and work? With focus, its beauty and significance will amplify.

We recently saw a film called *La La Land* about an aspiring actress and struggling jazz pianist in Los Angeles who have a tumultuous love affair, all the while encouraging each other to pursue their dreams. When the movie was over, I was poignantly struck with how in our marriages we often don't see the forest for the trees. When our needs aren't being met within the relationship, we often start looking outside our marriage for answers (options) when what we want we already have. We've just either lost, or have never developed, the eyesight to see it.

What we often need is a shift in perspective. We need a new pair of glasses through which to see our relationship. In fact, I'd like to suggest that you use the word "lover" in lieu of words like husband, wife, spouse, etc. It's a powerful demonstration of how vocabulary can change how you feel about something as well as its meaning. I like to use it because it alludes to eros love, and after all, this book is really about creating and nurturing deep love and passion in a marriage.

"What we often need is a shift in perspective. We need a new pair of glasses through which to see our relationship."

So how does one treat a "lover"? Lovingly, right? You treat them with affection; you frequently express your desire for them; you put them on a pedestal; you are endearing in your communications; you treat them like they are special. After all, the eros love that brought you together and will ultimately keep you together, is what makes your relationship special and different from all others.

Without eros, you are just friends, not lovers. Right? Is it easy to be impatient or unkind to a spouse, husband or wife? Yes. How about a lover? No way! You don't dare say or do something hurtful to a lover. If you do, you're very quick to make amends and seek reconciliation. Why? Because you don't want to lose them. Why? Because they fill a need! Hmmm. Since when did your spouse, um...lover, cease to be your lover? Since when did we start taking our lover for granted? When we got married? No. When we had kids? No. When life got overwhelming? No. Your lover ceased being your lover when you stopped treating them like your lover!

This could be the most important distinction in this book so don't miss it. It's not enough to intellectualize this information;

"Your lover ceased being your lover when you stopped treating them like your lover!"

you've got to internalize it. Contrary to popular belief, knowledge is NOT power. Knowledge is "potential" power. The power comes in using the knowledge, in putting it into practice and making it a part of your operating system. It's taking the Sunday morning sermon to work with you. It's honoring your God, yourself and your lover 24/7. It's acting with integrity and congruence. You can't completely love without integrity, and you can't really have integrity without love.

So let's turn the statement above into an affirmation you can take with you.

"I will love my lover (husband, wife) like a lover loves a lover."

Love is the universal language that bridges all gaps and transcends all barriers. Love, if completely exemplified in a marriage, makes everything else in this book a moot point. Expanding your personal definition of love and your capacity to embody and personify that love, by itself, can transform your marriage and your life. My own version of I Corinthians 13: 4-7 reads like this.

Love is energy. Love is our reason for being alive. Love is the source of all things. It is blissful and humorous. It is safe and warm. Love makes the complex seem simple. It is ever growing and expanding. Love is limitless and forever. It doesn't have conditions. It is mystical and magical. It's transcendent. Love is sacred and divine.

What do you think would happen if you chose daily to embody this kind of love in your relationships? If you saw your marriage as sacred and divine, how would that influence your thoughts and actions? If you embraced the idea that love is providing safety and warmth to another, how would that affect your perspective and your behavior toward your mate? What would happen if you found the comedy and humor in the circumstances that would ordinarily upset you? What if the greatest way for you to grow in love is to actually just keep growing, expanding and evolving yourself to a higher level of consciousness?

I challenge you to start seeing and appreciating the adventure, mystery and hilarity in your marriage and your lives. Find the grand purpose and meaning in the "challenges" you are facing. Look at things with more curiosity, wonder and expectation. Find the spark, the energy and the magic in your marriage. If you don't feel like you have any of these things, it's within your power to create them. Just asking myself, "How can I bring more adventure, comedy, mystery, hilarity, expectation, curiosity, romance and magic to my marriage?" gets me excited. I know that it will get me focused, invoke some appreciation and gratitude for what I have, as well as expand my capacity to love.

Is love all you need? No. Not in the context of an enduring, passionate marriage. See you in the next chapter.

ACTION STEPS

1. Recommit yourself to grow in love and love your mate at a whole new level. Step out and love them on their terms, according to their definition of what love means. Remember, marriage isn't a 50/50 proposition. It's 100/100! You give 100% all the time. You don't wait for your mate to take the first step. You don't wait for your mate to earn your love. You love them 100% all the time.

2. Consider how you can create a safe space where you and your mate can be more open and authentic without fear of judgment, criticism or withholding.

3. Treat you mate like a lover treats a lover.

IS LOVE ENOUGH?

I ENDED THE LAST chapter by asking the question "Is love all you need?" Another way of asking this is, "Is love enough?" One woman answered this question when she said, "I used to think that love was enough. But now I realize that I need to fall in love with my husband over and over."

Love used to be enough. Prior to the middle of the last century, the model for marriage was quite simple really. In fact, it was a model that had endured for thousands of years. Marriage was more of an arrangement than it was love affair or adventure. Women married for security and men married for sex, stature and propagation. Women cooked, cleaned and raised children while men provided food, shelter and defense. This isn't to say that marriage didn't have love. It often did, even if it was the kind that grew over time. Romantic love was not unheard of either, even if it faded over time.

Even through the latter part of the 20th century, the definitions some had of what it meant to be a good husband or wife were fairly one-dimensional. Being a good husband meant simply that a man provided well for his wife and family. Being a good wife meant that a woman kept the house, raised the kids, and made herself available to her husband once in a while.

This archaic model worked really well right up to the point where it didn't. We are now at one of those unique points in history where what we've done to get us where we are, isn't going to get us where we want to go. We've evolved and are more sophisticated at large. I think most people live at a higher level of consciousness than ever before, at least I want to believe that. We have higher expectations than ever in the history of mankind.

"We want to get married, but we don't want to lose the excitement and passion that comes with falling in love and being magnetized to someone."

We want security *and* adventure. We want certainty *and* variety. We want love *and* desire. We want to have the certainty of love and connection, but not at the sacrifice of desire and attraction. We want to get married, but we don't want to lose the excitement and passion that comes with falling in love and being magnetized to someone. Really wanting something or someone makes you feel alive. Being really wanted by someone makes you feel alive.

Marriages often end, not because of lack of love, but because of lack of attraction. You love each other but you don't *want* each other. You don't inspire, compel, challenge, magnetize or excite each other. Is the question "Is love enough?" a fair question to ask? I think most Christians would argue that it is. I would have to agree that love is enough if you really love completely and without limit. However, I'm guessing that most of us (me included) have a very limited and incomplete grasp on what it means to really love. With that said, if you want a passionate, life-long love affair that transcends our old model of a working/caring relationship where we more often than not settle for less than what we desire out of life, we need to maintain our attraction to each other.

The next section is about understanding and nurturing the 2nd Element in your marriage and that is the element of Polarity.

ACTION STEPS

1. Have a thoughtful review of your beliefs about whether love is enough, or should be enough, in your marriage?
2. If you do believe that love is enough, would your marriage have flourished more if you'd taken the approach of never resting on your laurels?

SECTION 2:
POLARITY

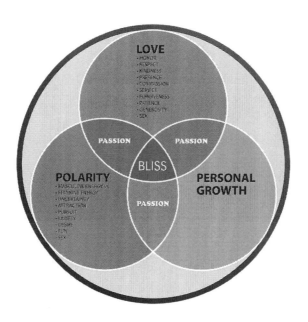

YIN/YANG

In Section 1, we learned about what it means to love at a deep level. We explored explicit and implicit vows and how consciously keeping them can transform your marriage through a deeper sense of awareness. We learned what the 7 core needs are and how supporting your mate in meeting those needs is loving them more completely than you may have ever imagined; and how meeting those needs bonds and endears them to you like never before. And then we questioned whether love is actually enough to keep a couple engaged in an enduring and fulfilling relationship. The answer to this question is different today than it would have been, say 50 or 60 years ago. Up until about 200 years ago, love wasn't even an expected or required component of marriage. However, today we have higher standards and expectations for what we get out of marriage. And if these expectations aren't met, we feel an unprecedented freedom, or even right, to abandon the commitment and look elsewhere to have unfulfilled needs met.

This brings us to the 2nd Element of the passionate marriage trifecta. Section 2 is all about the Element of Polarity. At the heart of polarity lies a most fundamental reality that in the beginning magnetizes men and women together, and often in the end drives them apart. And that reality is that men and women are different. So different in fact, that Dr. John Gray conceived the analogy of men being from Mars and women being from Venus.

In case this messed up world has confused your perception of reality, men and women are very different. We don't look the same. At least we aren't supposed to. It's hard to tell who is what anymore. We don't think the same way. We don't feel the same way. We don't react the same way. We don't internalize things the same way. We don't process things the same way. We don't remember things the same way. We don't love the same and don't need to be loved the same. We often just don't see things the same. It's no wonder the gods are busting a gut up there. They've created the ultimate romance/comedy/drama.

My WTF Comedy/Drama

A comical demonstration of the masculine/feminine difference happened one day when Kimberly and I were discussing how certain behaviors in a spouse can incite intense emotional responses such as anger, frustration, impatience, and total bewilderment. The context of the conversation was really about the idea that negative responses to challenging behaviors are actually opportunities for the "responder" to do a self-check In other words, when you're feeling upset with your mate, it's your opportunity to work on "state" management and maybe even reassess your "broken" rules that got you upset in the first place.

The example that came up was of how often there is contention amongst couples over being on time to appointments, engagements or dates and how often one of you is ready to go "on time" and the other is late in getting ready. In case you thought you were special, this happens to us all the time.

So I decide to paint a scenario. Now bear in mind that I'm stereotyping the situation and any resemblance it might have to our real life is purely coincidental. Ironically, the more hypothetical I tried to make it, the closer to home it seemed to hit. Anyway, as you read, note that the roles could, for some couples, be reversed. However, in my household, the stereotype holds true.

The Scenario

- Our couple has a 6 PM dinner engagement with another couple at one of the hardest to get into restaurants in town.
- He is ready to go at 5:30 PM.
- They need 15 minutes to get there. Translation: They need to leave by probably 5:40 PM to allow time for parking and walking to the restaurant.
- At 5:30 PM, he hollers upstairs saying "Baby, we need to leave by 5:40 PM, 5:45 PM at the latest to be there on time" to which she retorts, "I'm getting ready as fast as I can."
- All the while he's thinking, "No, you're getting ready as fast as *you* want!"
- 5:45 PM comes and goes and so does 6:00 PM.
- By the time she comes down the stairs at 6:10 PM, he's a little steamed.

It's not that he minds eating a little later, it's that his rules about being on time have been broken.

- He's been thinking, "I don't want anyone to have to wait for me. It's rude. After all, I'm a man of my word and when I tell someone I'll be someplace at a given time, I'm going to be there!" "Besides, I don't want to fall into disfavor with the restaurant." "Can't she give herself enough time to get ready?" "This is embarrassing."
- Well, according to this "hypothetical" scenario, they leave the house at 6:15 PM and arrive at the restaurant at 6:30 PM.
- Because he doesn't want to be any later, he opts to have the car valet parked so they can walk right in.

Kimberly's response to the scenario

- "So Tad, if the couple got to the restaurant at 6:30, but he was ready to leave the house at 5:30 PM, was *he* really late?"
- She continues, "He's not late if he was ready to go on time but prevented from doing so by someone else."
- To which I respond with my mouth hanging open and a look of dumb bewilderment on my face.

Kimberly continues

- "If the other couple was also 30 minutes late, were you actually late?"
- And then she says, "If you arrived at the engagement late but nobody cared that you were late, are you really late?"
- At this point I don't know whether to laugh or cry because I feel like my head is about to explode.
- And then finishes with, "I think that whether you're late or not is more about your ego and your concern about what other people think than about being on time".

After that I was seeing stars. It blew my friggin' mind. It made me crazy. And then I suddenly started busting *my* gut. A natural progression don't you think? I wasn't laughing my head off because I thought Kimberly was out in left field but because I realized how wonderfully and beautifully different we are. I got a glimpse of how our world can expand when we embrace our inherent differences. It's no longer about who's right and who's wrong, it's about growing our frame of reference by appreciating, entertaining and honoring our differences; especially in how we view the world.

When you learn to do this, you'll do a lot more laughing and a lot less crying. If you could actually anticipate one of these comedic, mind-altering exchanges, you could make some popcorn and make an evening out of it!

The Yin and Yang of It

Most relationship problems come from men and women thinking and acting like we're the same. We're clearly not! Our differences attracted us together in the first place and are largely responsible for driving us out of our minds later on.

So what happens? Why do a man and woman (total opposites) fall in love and then get frustrated with their differences, fight over their differences, and often get divorced over their differences? The answer is simple. They don't realize that their differences, and the conflict those differences seem to cause, are actually blessings in disguise, and evidence that they are probably perfectly compatible. They don't understand, appreciate, embrace and nurture their polarity. They don't get that this is the way it is meant to be and that it's all good!

In Chinese philosophy, yin and yang describe what seem to be opposite forces that actually complement each other. In fact, they are interdependent and cannot exist without the other. Each has no meaning without the contrast that the other provides. Examples of this are night and day, good and evil, positive and negative, black and white, hot and cold, and of course, male and female.

As women and men, we often fail to recognize, acknowledge, and appreciate the significance of the fact that we are polar opposites. This failure is responsible for a lot of our grief. A helpful illustration of this is to imagine a man and woman standing back-to-back on the beach in California. The man is facing east (toward land) and the woman is facing west (toward the ocean). The kicker is that their backs are permanently connected, they can't turn their heads, they were born this way, in this spot, and have never moved. Now, how do you think their perspectives on the same world will differ? One will have never seen but only a non-descript hint of an ocean even though it is right behind them, and the other will have never seen but only the vaguest suggestion of land and mountains even though it is right behind them. One will have never seen the sun rise, the other will have never seen a sun set; though each will have experienced the evidence of each. Because of their orientation, they will each likely favor a different time of day, and for good reason. If they chose to argue about what the world looked like from their own partial perceptions of reality, there would be unending conflict. If they chose instead to honor and embrace each other's differing points of view and seem their perspectives together, they would each have a more beautiful, colorful, and accurate experience of the world. In other words, it takes both of you, together, to get a clear picture of the true nature of things. If you were both the same, one of you wouldn't be needed.

Irreconcilable Differences

I think it's hilarious that the most commonly stated reason for divorce is "irreconcilable differences". I think this because the differences will always be there. If they went away, your marriage would die from boredom and loss of attraction. In most cases, the only reason for "irreconcilable differences" is the refusal by one or both to change the perspective and meaning they place on those differences. This requires personal growth. If you don't change, you will have irreconcilable differences with anyone you marry.

Men and women are like vinegar and oil, distinctly different. One is acidic and harsh, the other smooth and silky. However, when combined, they complement each other perfectly. When emulsified with real love, they are inseparable. This phenomenon happens when true love is demonstrated through our support of our mate's 7 core needs, the cultivation of the natural polarity between us, and our own never-ending personal growth.

I hope you're digesting this important point! If you're doing this right, you will have problems. That's a good thing. Another way to look at these experiences are as opportunities to challenge yourself and grow.

Love, and the certainty that comes with true love, is what makes a marriage good. But love isn't what makes a marriage exciting, inspiring and really rewarding. Join me in the next chapter as I reveal the second secret to a passionate marriage.

ACTION STEPS

Take a moment to consider some upsetting situations between you and your spouse that may be a reflection of your Yin and Yang differences. How different does it feel when you look at your differences with honor and appreciation? When you remember that it's your inherent differences that attracted you together in the first place, it's easier to appreciate the critical role they play in your relationship. When you acknowledge that your mate has a legitimate perspective on things that is simply different than yours, your world will grow and magnify as you incorporate it into your reality. It's really all quite a laughing matter. Start looking for the comedy in everything and start laughing instead of yelling or getting angry.

POLARITY

AN OFT-REPEATED CONCEPT IN this book is that a good marriage is good right up to the point when it's not. I don't throw this concept around to scare you or make you uneasy. I do it to wake you out of complacency. The implication here is that "good" may not be good enough to keep a couple together over the long haul.

Here's why. If a marriage isn't "passionate" or "outstanding", that implies that something is missing and that some need or needs are not being met. Usually when a couple says that their marriage is good, they invariably mean "good enough". But good enough may not really be good enough because "good enough" usually describes one's willingness to settle or make-do. "Good enough" is often acceptable when life is crazy and there's no energy left to put into your relationship. But "good enough" is only good enough until one or both parties in the relationship, at some point in time, decide that they don't want to settle for less than what they really want or need! This might mean that they are tired of their needs not being met in the relationship or maybe they really miss the spontaneity, variety, uncertainty and passion they had in the beginning and they want it back. They want to feel that lovin' feeling again. They want to feel alive.

"Most good relationships have plenty of "love", but what they lack is passion." This is important to understand because it underscores the answer to the question, "Is love enough?" Love should be enough but most people don't love fully and completely. I would like to suggest that keeping our vows *is* to love fully and completely, which means honoring our commitment to help our mate meet their 7 core needs at a high level. Most people in "good" marriages meet some of these needs, usually the ones they feel comfortable meeting. It's the needs that go unmet that rear their heads unexpectedly to throw you for a loop. Most good relationships have plenty of "love", but what they lack is passion. Love gives you certainty and certainty can make a rela-

tionship work. But a working relationship isn't a passionate relationship. It just plain sucks when you're committed to someone who you love, but are no longer attracted to.

This brings me to 3 questions asked by Esther Perel in her book *Mating In Captivity*. "Can we desire what we already have?" "Can we have both love and desire in the same relationship over time?" and "What exactly would that kind of relationship be?" My answers to the first 2 questions are yes and yes. My answer to the 3rd question is what this book is all about. It's about how to have a passionate, enduring relationship where attraction and desire thrive.

The 2nd Element for a passionate marriage is polarity. Polarity is opposite poles attracting each other. Polarity is what enamors you to the opposite sex. It's what instigates the infatuation and euphoria experienced in courtship. Polarity keeps you coming back for more. It's the "can't live without 'em" part of the old adage we all know by heart. However, if you implement the principles in this book, the "you can't live with 'em" part will change. Polarity is what makes a marriage passionate. Polarity, and the sex you have as a result of it, is the primary thing that makes marriage different from all other relationships. Without passion and sex, all you have is a contractual "working" relationship. There are exceptions to this rule, but they are rare.

"Love gives you certainty and certainty can make a relationship work. But a 'working' relationship isn't a passionate relationship. It just plain sucks when you're committed to someone who you love but are no longer attracted to."

Remember the 7 core needs? The first was the need for certainty. The second was the need for uncertainty. Notice that these are opposing needs, but still both valid needs nonetheless. One of the ways our need for certainty is met, is through the love and commitment we have to each other. However, if the need for *uncertainty* (which can also be described as our need for variety and excitement) isn't met, the relationship becomes stale, boring and monotonous over time. A couple may be fully committed to each other and never part, but that doesn't mean their needs are being met within the relationship. A good relationship has love and certainty while a passionate relationship *also* has polarity and a healthy element of uncertainty.

"Uncertainty is a natural byproduct of men and women living true to their masculine and feminine energies. It's crucial that we support these core essences in ourselves and in each other."

Uncertainty is a natural byproduct of men

and women living true to their masculine and feminine energies. It's crucial that we support these core essences in ourselves and in each other. We can do that by embracing, honoring, appreciating and supporting our natural differences, no matter how mind blowing they might seem at times. If we attempt to diminish these differences, all we succeed in doing is diminishing our attraction and desire for each other.

Kimberly, our daughter and I went to Disneyworld in Orlando Florida this last spring break. We stayed at a Disney resort called Port Orleans Riverside that had a New Orleans theme to it. When we checked in it was dark, cold and a little rainy which made us a little anxious to get settled into our room. At check-in, the receptionist provided us with a map and instructions to get to our room which was in another building on the other side of an adjacent river. The instructions were, "Go back outside through the front door you came in, turn left, follow the sidewalk to the river, cross the bridge, turn right, and your building will be right there."

Well, since we arrived at close to 9:00 PM without having had dinner, we decided to go get a bite before going to our room. So we dragged our luggage through the main hotel building in search of a suitable restaurant. An hour or so later, we had full tummies but were very tired and anxious to get to the room. So, we headed for the front door. I was in the lead with the family in tow. We get outside and I turn to the left as instructed and start heading in what I believe to be the correct direction to get to our building. Kimberly, who is a very independent thinker, stops me and says, "This doesn't look right. I think we were supposed to turn right." To which I retort, "No, we're supposed to turn left, follow the sidewalk to the river and cross the river." To which she responds, "We're not supposed to cross a river! This doesn't look right. Let's go ask a bellman how to get there." So we walk up to a bellman who proceeds to tell us to go exactly where I was taking us.

I have to admit that I was a little irked because I felt like she was questioning my memory, my judgment, and my leadership.

Later, after we went to bed, Kimberly snuggles up to me and says, "Are you still mad at me? Don't be mad at me. Please forgive me." To which I replied, "I'm not mad. I just feel depolarized from you." I was feeling a loss of attraction to her at that moment. She then responded with, "You shouldn't feel depolarized, you were entirely right and I was entirely wrong. If that's not polarity, I don't know what is?" This broke my frustrated state and we both broke out laughing.

I acknowledge my man's need to lead and we have very definitive roles in our relationship where we concede to the other's best judgment. For example, I'm in charge of our home and our daughter. It's helpful and more productive to have a designated or acknowledged leader in most instances; remembering most great leaders consult their high council (i.e., their mate) when applicable and make their decisions in consideration of the couple's best interest.

Sometimes people ask, "How can 2 people live together if they are opposites in every way?" The answer is that they can't be opposite in every way. This is where I want to draw a distinction between polarity differences and values differences. What gives a marriage a solid foundation is being in alignment with your values, goals, ambitions, dreams and spiritual beliefs. These things aren't masculine or feminine in nature. Being in alignment doesn't mean you have to completely agree with each other on these things, but that your core governing values are compatible. That ensures that you are moving through life together close enough to do it holding hands. Goals, ambitions and dreams, when governed by common values, can then be encouraged and supported. However, when there is misalignment in a couple's values, there is often a lot of compromise, and compromise leads to resentment. In Section 3, I'm going to share with you how a couple can deal with goals, dreams, or preferences that are a mismatch, and how that can actually strengthen their relationship.

Masculine and Feminine Energies

Masculine energy is all about focus, problem solving, conquering and getting things done. Masculine energy takes the biggest problems and tries to make them as small as possible. The masculine is analytical, purposeful and confident. It exudes immovable strength and integrity that make the feminine feel safe and secure. A masculine man craves a feminine woman.

As women we need to embrace men's hunter/warrior spirit and remember how these skills protect and provide for us. This beautiful, masculine DNA is what enabled the human race to survive and is a perfect complement to our feminine when we allow it to be.

Feminine energy on the other hand is fluid, deep and powerful, kind of like the ocean. It's full of endless possibilities, but generally lacks focus, dancing from place to place and thought to thought. Feminine energy tends to make small problems much bigger than they really are. It sees everything as a connected whole. The feminine *is* life itself. The feminine woman is magnetized to a masculine man.

The feminine energy is not only demonstrated in how we think but how we move through space, and how we interact with our mate and others.

I remember an extremely painful experience from 2001 that demonstrates the significance of polarity and how it affects attraction. One day my husband told me he didn't find me attractive. I said to myself, "What! I'm a hottie! Is he crazy? How could this be possible?" After pondering his statement for a couple of weeks I came to the conclusion that it had nothing to do with how I looked, but rather it was the role I was playing at work. The work I was doing was distinctly masculine in nature requiring me to suppress my feminine energy while accentuating my masculine. Good for the job but bad for our polarity. I learned to choose roles in my work that supported our polarity and to stay in my feminine for that is where my true power is.

Sixteen years later I find it a great compliment that my lover tells me he thinks I'm hotter than ever.

Here is a good place to throw in a little disclaimer. I make generalizations about the dynamics and polarity between men and women that apply to roughly 80 percent of relationships. If you are one of the 10 to 20 percent of men or women whose dominant essence is not masculine or feminine respectively, the rules and principles still apply, just in reverse. There is almost always a predominantly masculine and predominantly feminine figure in any marriage. However, they do not always fall into traditional roles as we know them. My point is that this does not in any way discount the significance of maintaining a healthy polarity in your relationship. The old cliché that opposites attract is oh, so true.

That said, some couples don't have strong polarity from the very beginning. However, they don't have passionate, deeply rewarding relationships either. No judgment intended. If 2 equally dispassionate people get together, they can have a good working, and even loving, relationship. It just won't have the kind of dynamic that inspires them to grow as individuals and as a couple.

Political Correctness (PC)

I really have a distaste for PC. Especially when it comes to how we have eliminated gender specific titles. I mean, come on! The same logic that gave us "servers" instead of waitresses and "flight attendants" in place of stewardesses will next eliminate gender specific names. Soon there will be no Robertas, just Bobs; no Kimberlys, just Kims. Taylor and Joey will be (are) the new "safe" names for the boys and girls of parents who choose to speculate about the *future* gender of their kid. I am really scared! That said, I think the elimination of gender specific titles has contributed to a new unintended consequence— the blurring of the sexes.

The woman's power movement in the 1940's; the feminist movement beginning in the 1960's and continuing today; the hippy movement of the 1960's; and the general desire of women to be independent have contributed to sexual neutrality in terms of polar attraction. I don't have anything against women's equality in society, to the contrary. It's just that when it comes to gender equality and polarity, the proverbial baby has been thrown out with the bath water.

A big problem is that in today's two-income family model, it's difficult to have polarity when he and she are both career oriented and take turns with the kids, meals, dishes, etc. In this scenario, polarity is lost because the lines between traditional roles have become blurred. The blurring of the lines between sexes is epidemic. Women are wearing pantsuits to the office in traditionally masculine roles, while men are staying at home, going to yoga, and driving the kids to and from after-school lessons.

The ugly truth of the matter is that women's and men's *natures* support more traditional roles, and not so much contemporary ones. As this book is not a treatise on human nature, I am speaking in generalizations. History, anthropology, social studies and current surveys prove this.

Men (masculine men) generally speaking, are attracted to women who exhibit feminine qualities and features. They want a woman who looks healthy and fertile with an hourglass figure and childbearing attri-

"The ugly truth of the matter is that women's and men's natures support more traditional roles, and not so much contemporary ones."

butes. They are magnetized to women whose energy makes them feel strong, capable and significant. Am I right? Men prefer a woman who makes them feel manly; a woman they feel they can protect and be a hero for. A woman that they can make happy! You can be the most physically beautiful specimen of a woman, but if you're impossible to make happy, no man will want to live with you. In fact, it will be hard for you to live with yourself.

When a woman demonstrates signs of happiness or being pleased with her man's efforts, this encouragement will motivate him to please you even more. If he can never please you, then eventually he will give up trying to please you. No one wants to play a game where they never win!

In contrast, most women innately want a man they perceive can provide for them, take care of them, and protect them. They want a guy who is strong and capable. They want a man who makes them feel like a woman.

Am I stereotyping men and women? Most certainly. But don't get me wrong. I think by now you know that I'm 110 percent in support of equality of the sexes, and I honor women above all else in this world. It's just hard for there to be any passion in a marriage when she's spent the day litigating a wrongful-death case or spent the day in the operating room, and he's spent the day chauffeuring the kids around to soccer and ballet. I don't think I'm off-base here, do you? I hope you detect the fun and maybe a little exaggeration here, but it is done to make a point.

When a man engages in roles that nurture his feminine side and his wife engages in roles that nurture her masculine side, what do you think is going to happen? In other words, if his feminine side is enhanced and his masculine side is diminished, and her masculine side is enhanced while her feminine side is diminished, what's the result? You can have a radical depolarization. You can have dramatically diminished attraction. You have essentially neutralized the very dynamic that attracted you together in the first place. It's not hard to see why so many couples today suffer from sexless marriages. The depolarization of married couples is largely responsible for break-ups today. When you lose your attraction and desire for someone and are not regularly connecting with them sexually, disconnection happens, tempers get short, and needs stop being met, if they ever were.

"The depolarization of married couples is largely responsible for break-ups today. When you lose your attraction and desire for someone and are not regularly connecting with them sexually, disconnection happens, tempers get short, and needs stop being met, if they ever were."

Society's desire to homogenize the sexes drives me crazy. Why can't men and women be true to their natures? Men and women must be true to their natures. Our personal power comes from being authentic; true to the essence of who we naturally are. Femininity does not equate to weakness, nor does masculinity necessarily equate to insensitivity. A man shoveling snow off the driveway while his lady is baking apple pie isn't a demonstration of inequality, it's an exemplification of our polar differences.

And just to be clear, a woman wearing a pantsuit to the office doesn't make her masculine any more than a man taking his daughter to gymnastics gets feminized. A feminine woman can wear anything and look feminine. It's all about energy. A woman is de-feminized when she must diminish her core essence and nurture her masculine side to be effective at her job. Let's face it, there are jobs, careers and expertise that are inherently masculine or feminine in terms of the energy required to do a good job. At the risk of offending someone, I think we could probably agree that it takes masculine energy to be a good trial lawyer or surgeon. And we both agree that there are darn good female trial lawyers and surgeons, maybe even the best. However, it's also our experience that there is often a greatly diminished polarity in their marriages.

There is power in the feminine that many women don't get to enjoy the benefit of because at some point they were sold a bill of goods that the masculine was better, stronger or smarter. However, I've personally experienced the power of the feminine to be my greatest resource in working in a male-dominated industry.

If this is you, you both need to regularly engage in activities that accentuate your sexual and polar differences. After all, desire is born from the "space" between you and your mate's polar differences. When those differences get blurred, polarity is lost and desire wanes.

When you don't desire the one you are with, it's inherently tempting to look elsewhere for the experience of "desire." I want to say this a different way. Humans have a need for desire. It's a secondary need, but

> *"...desire is born from the "space" between you and your mate's polar differences. When those differences get blurred, polarity is lost and desire wanes."*

a need nonetheless. We simply desire to desire. It feels really good to really want something. It's a juicy sensation. It's the feeling of aliveness. We not only want to be wanted but we have a craving to crave something or someone. When desire is diminished or lost within a committed relationship, we become vulnerable to spontaneously experiencing desire for someone outside

> *"We not only want to be wanted but we have a craving to crave something or someone."*

the relationship. And because desire is such a powerful and addictive emotion, it can easily lure you down a road that doesn't support your marriage.

What to Do?

So, what does this all mean in practical terms? What are you supposed to do to support the polarity in your marriage?

First off, remember that polarity is the dynamic between 2 opposing energies. If you experienced physical attraction to each other in the beginning, then one of you is predominately feminine at the core and the other masculine. Maintaining your polarity is more about nurturing these energies than it is about what you wear or what your career choice is, although that can be part of it. That said, the trending homogenization of men's and women's roles in society makes it more challenging and even more crucial to nurture polarity with intention. Historically, polarity came easy. Traditional roles naturally supported it. Men were men and women were women. There was never any confusion between the two in any regard. Now, we've got our work cut out for us. If you feel a loss of attraction and desire for your mate, it could just be that you have lost your polarity.

Getter or Gettee? In *The Way of the Superior Man*, David Deida points out that every passionate relationship needs a ravisher and a "ravishee". In other words, there needs to be a pursuer and "pursuee"; a hunter and the hunted. In our relationship it was getter and "gettee". I "get" my wife and she always wanted to be "got". Whenever there is any chasing going on in the bedroom, I am always the one doing the chasing, never the other way around. I think you can read between the lines.

If you want "equality" in the bedroom, you might as well just sign the death warrant for any attraction and desire you might have. When I say equality, I really mean sameness of energy and how that energy is expressed. It really helps if you aren't built the same as well. Are an Oak tree and a Pine tree equal? They're both trees. The fact of the matter is that they are equally valuable but for very different reasons. An Oak tree's wood is very hard, a Pine tree's very soft. Oak has a quality that stands up to wear and tear making it suitable for furniture and flooring. Pine is malleable and flexible making it easy to work with and historically perfect for the masts of ships. Oak is hard to burn but once started puts out more heat than Pine. Pine is easy to start a fire with but burns up quickly. Honoring the differences means playing to the strengths and weaknesses of each.

Let's face it, pretending that men can do what women do and vice versa is folly. Men are stronger, faster and have more stamina than women, generally speaking. That's why men and women don't compete against each other in sports. It's not a question of equality, it's a question of "different". Women are softer, more sensitive, more intuitive, often smarter, more pain tolerant, and more nurturing. Again, I'm speaking in generalizations so don't shut down if this doesn't apply to you perfectly.

That said, if you cling to politically correct notions of sameness, especially in the bedroom, you will have a radical depolarization. Not only does this affect your attraction and desire for each other as a couple, but not living congruent with your natural essence will make it impossible to truly feel fulfilled at your core. No matter whether you are masculine or feminine at your core, if you have had to amplify your polar opposite energy to be successful at your chosen career, you may have sacrificed your authentic self for success.

In other words, if you have a feminine core but have to function with masculine energy to be good at your job, you won't be fulfilled unless you are capable of stepping out of the masculine and back into the feminine when you get home. If you want

"No matter whether you are masculine or feminine at your core, if you have had to amplify your polar opposite energy to be successful at your chosen career, you may have sacrificed your authentic self for success."

the possibility of a passionate love affair and deep fulfillment in your life, you've got to live congruent with who you are at your core. You've got to be true to yourself.

For me, it's doing my best to interact and make decisions from my heart and out of a place of love. You can wear whatever hat fulfills you outside the home, but when it comes to your family, words and actions with love at their core will evoke the perfect balance to the male energy.

So what do you do?

Get re-acquainted with your core energy. If you are for some reason confused about this, here are a few simple test questions that will help you identify whether you are masculine or feminine at the core.

1. If you weren't with your mate on Sunday night, would you prefer to watch football or Cupcake Wars?
2. If no one was looking would you drink Cabernet Sauvignon or White Zinfandel?
3. Action movie or a drama?
4. Casino Royale or Golden Eye?
5. Bull riding or barrel racing?

6. Chopping wood or baking pie?
7. Did you like dodgeball when you were a kid?
8. Are you a natural ravisher or "ravishee"?

To answer these questions honestly, you have to look beyond the mask that you might be wearing to what is underneath in your core being. What kind of activities did you gravitate to when you were a child? Were they inherently masculine or feminine?

Since childhood, we have often adopted behaviors and personas that are not authentically us in order to be what we think we need to be to be enough, to be loved, to be accepted, and to be less vulnerable. We often even choose careers, not because they resonate with us, but because we think it will help us get the love and/or respect of someone whose love we crave. However, when we do this, we are living a lie. And when you live a lie, you will never be truly fulfilled. Get in touch with the YOU that is your heart and soul and learn to live there. That is where life is for you.

Honor and nurture your differences. Your differences are what attracted you to each other in the beginning and will help you maintain real attraction and polarity throughout your marriage. However, you must focus on the differences that attract you to your mate and de-focus on the differences that make you want to hang yourself. The differences that figuratively make you want to cut your own throat were always there in the beginning; you just didn't notice them because you were "doped up" with chemicals that exist in your body to ensure the survival of the human race. You were seeing everything with rose-colored glasses. These special glasses are compliments of a sweet little love potion that your body produced when you were courting. This chemical elixir made up of serotonin, oxytocin and dopamine tends to wear off after about 18 months, leaving you kind of spinning and wondering, *what the heck is happening*? (BTW: we will explore how to reintroduce this chemical love cocktail back into your relationship later in the book.)

"Your differences are what attracted you to each other in the beginning and will help you maintain real attraction and polarity throughout your marriage."

Your mate's little habits, nuances, and perspectives on things now seem to bug the living crap out of you. This is your cue to immediately de-focus on all the stuff that drives you crazy, and start consciously focusing on what you love about your mate and worshipping those qualities. Honor their feminine or masculine essence. Show them respect for who they are, and let them know through your words and actions that they don't have to change a thing to feel honored by you. Remember the short list of innate differences between the sexes earlier in this chapter. Trust me, you don't want to change those. You've got to let go, smile to yourself, and say, "You know, I'm really blessed to have a little crazy in my life." Put those rose-colored glasses back on and start seeing your mate as they really are—wonderfully and beautifully made. All the trivial differences are just that, trivial.

Stop thinking that you have to understand your mate. You won't always understand. You may never understand. It's OK! But that doesn't make them wrong. It just makes them different. Revel in it. Bask in it. Honor it. A little bit of crazy will polarize you together.

If you are a man, start cultivating your masculinity. (If you're a woman, please skip to the next section). This is *huge* because it is ultimately your manhood that coaxes your lady's womanhood out of hiding. She wants a man who compels her to love and admire him. A feminine woman wants a man that knows what he wants and goes after it. She craves to be taken care of. She doesn't want to have to make all the important decisions. She needs you to take responsibility in a way that allows her to relax into her femininity. The more you do this, the more freedom she'll feel to be in her essence, the essence that attracted you to her in the first place. Take control of getting things done. Get that darn honey-do list done. Take a load off her plate. Give her some breathing room. Tell her you want her. Do innately masculine things that get you in touch with your manhood, while making her feel you are strong and capable of protecting and providing for her. Have a load of un-split firewood delivered to the house and start splitting it with a big maul. Change the oil in your/her car yourself. Start working out if you don't already. Stand up for yourself at times when you might normally allow yourself to be taken advantage of. Grow a beard. Shave your beard. If she suspiciously asks what's going on, tell her you decided you want to look good for her...because she deserves it!

And maybe more than anything, show her that you are unshakeable. She needs to know that no matter what happens, you're not going to fall apart, explode, melt down, give up or withdraw.

Here is one of the great dichotomies and paradoxes of women. They want what they want, they want you to know what they want, and they want you to give them what they want. But sometimes what they really want isn't what they want at all, but something much deeper than what they reveal on the surface.

At the core we want to be loved, and appreciated, and respected. We want to know that we hold the key to your heart.

It's hard for me to write this without laughing out loud because this is what drives men out of their minds. Women are testing creatures. They are constantly testing your love, attraction, and commitment to them in often subtle ways. One of the unconscious ways they do this is by making requests and demands that test your manhood. What they are saying they want on the surface is not really what they want. What they want is to know that you are a man they can respect and trust, and who is congruent.

She wants to know that you will give her or help her achieve her heart's desire. Most of the time your willingness to participate in this effort is what she wants most, not necessarily achieving the end result but going on this journey, adventure or pursuit with her.

They want you to demonstrate that you will live true to your core, true to your calling, true to your higher purpose in life. Because that's what a man does, and she wants a real man in her life. That said, a real man will live his higher purpose and do it while meeting his wife's needs on a high level.

A women wants a man that confides in her; that shares his dreams, joys, concerns and fears. This is part of being intimate with a women. If you are bothered by your work, the kids or financial problems and you work alone to solve them she feels excluded, and withholding your feelings creates an emotional barrier.

If you're a woman, honor, embrace, and embody your femininity. This is your beauty, your magic, and your power. A masculine man craves a feminine woman. When I was in college, I read a book that suggested that all progress historically, was inspired by a man's desire for a woman, his need to impress a woman or his need to take care of his woman. I don't know how true that is but I can say one thing for sure, it is true for me. I wouldn't be the man I am today if it wasn't for my desire to have, keep, hold, and impress the feminine woman in my life. Feminine energy gives a man hope, a reason. He feeds on it. It is a source of life for him. He experiences this energy in your softness, your tenderness, your vulnerability, and even more so, in your movement. It emanates from your eyes and through your skin. Even the plainest face becomes beautiful when your inner radiance shines. Feminine energy radiates in the movement, flow and dance of a woman. Why do you think men the world over pay to watch women dance? It's to bask themselves in the soothing salve and vitalizing, light feminine energy. Some women may think that to dance for a man is subservient and demeaning. Is a man on the front lines of a war zone subservient to the women and children he is fighting to protect? Is a husband demeaned because he is chosen as a suitable mate based on his physical prowess, education or intelligence? Is it demeaning to serve one another; to offer each the polar gifts that make us so uniquely different and magnetizing to each other? Au contraire.

Men today know you can take care of yourself. They know you don't need them anymore. You've more than proven that. And maybe somewhere in the process you've managed to suppress at least a little (if not a lot) of your true essence. An unintended consequence of this is that men have felt emasculated. Your power and independence doesn't diminish our built-in need and desire to take care of you, protect you, provide for you and be a hero for you.

We *need* to be your hero. We need to be able to rescue you once in a while or our need for significance won't be filled. Nothing can light a man up like a woman's genuine smile; her belief in him that he can accomplish anything he puts his mind to; her respect and trust in his intentions, decisions and actions.

Romance. Romance is such a big part of polarity and having a passionate marriage that it deserves its own space. I'll see you in the next chapter.

ACTION STEPS

1. Consider whether you have sacrificed your true nature to fit into your various roles, at work or at home.
2. Identify your core energy. What would change if you could be your true self with your partner?
3. What can you do to nurture your naturally masculine or feminine energies? How can you nurture the natural energies of your mate?
4. Witness the masculine/feminine polarity between Kimberly and I on our weekly video blog posts by going to www.GreatMarriageGreatLife.com.

IT'S ALL ABOUT THE CHASE

RECAPPING A LITTLE FROM the last chapter, for there to be polarity (attraction and desire) in your relationship, there must be a ravisher and ravishee, or a pursuer and pursuee. This is the dynamic behind all courtship and romance.

Traditionally (maybe 80% of the time), it is the man who pursues the woman, but not always. Sometimes (maybe 20% of the time), the woman is the dominant masculine energy and it's the man who feels the need to be wooed. It's in our DNA to either be a hunter or the hunted; a getter or a get-tee; masculine or feminine. Historically, traditionally and anthropologically speaking, men are looking for a woman who is worthy of their pursuit while women are looking (or waiting) for a man who is worthy to entrust their virtues to. When we find someone who seems worthy, we go through a testing and wooing process to determine if they are suitable and win them over to us. We call this process courtship—at least we used to. Maybe it's an archaic term now but it's the best we've got.

Courtship and the romance that usually accompanies it, too often end with the marriage ceremony. After all, we got our prize. Now we can go on with our lives, focusing on our careers, raising kids and preparing for retirement. Right?

OK, OK, you know all this. I'm not telling you anything new. "Just tell me how to keep the romance alive in my marriage!" you might be saying.

Well, I'm not going to try and tell you how to romance your partner or incite romance from your partner. You know how to do that already. You just don't do it. Remember the chapter on psychology? The problem that most people have, isn't that they don't know what to do, it's getting themselves to do it. It's really all about mindset and perspective. Sometimes all we need is a paradigm shift, or a shift in perspective, and instantly everything just seems more clear. This is what did it for me.

In his book *Flow*, Mihaly Csikszentmihalyi made a powerful statement that influenced the polar dynamic between Kimberly and me forever. Here it is. Read it slowly at least twice.

> *Goals justify the effort they demand at the outset, but later it is the effort that justifies the goal. One gets married because the spouse seems worthy of sharing one's life with, but unless one then behaves as if this is true, the partnership will appear to lose value with time.*

This is one of the most powerful statements I have ever read. It's telling us 2 things—first, that the quality of our marriage is a manifestation of the effort we put into it; and more significantly, our marriage is only as good as the value we place on it. In the beginning we pursued our mate because we believed they were worth pursuing. But unless we continue to treat them as a worthy pursuit, their value to us will diminish with time.

"In the beginning we pursued our mate because we believed they were worth pursuing. But unless we continue to treat them as a worthy pursuit, their value to us will diminish with time."

Magic occurs when we treat our mate as the most important person in our life and our marriage as the most important relationship. When you "act as if", your relationship evolves to the very thing you seek. Carefully make decisions and choices that support each other and your life together with thoughtful consideration. Small efforts and gestures will become habit, and a reciprocity of these efforts between the two of you will manifest a life-long love affair.

This is the paradox of achievement. We tend to justify the journey by the destination; or the process of achievement by the goal. However, once the destination is reached, if one doesn't set new goals so as to re-engage in the "process", the goals become meaningless. Life is all about the journey and so is marriage.

The old model of marriage gives us up to 24 months of courtship and romantic bliss followed by a life of diminishing romance, diminishing sex and diminishing fulfillment. The new model we have for you will give you a life of perpetual romance, enhanced polarity, fulfilling love and connection, and mind-blowing sex.

This chapter is called "It's all about the chase" because that's what polarity and romance is all about. In our house, we have often chased each other around the bedroom as a ritual for getting into "state" for making love. My physical pursuit of her while she's playing hard-to-get unfailingly magnifies our masculine/feminine energies, puts us right into the moment, gets our hearts pumping, our bodies oxygenated and usually induces laughter, if not hysteria. The reason I share this intimate vignette of our personal life is because it illustrates the importance of the chase. Pursuing my wife makes me want her more. Being pursued by me makes her feel wanted and consequently want me more. Romance is all about pursuing and being pursued. It's kind of like the game of cat and mouse. Kimberly pursues me by doing the very things that would attract me as a pursuer. She baits me, intrigues me and mystifies me. She does this largely by cultivating her femininity and continuing to grow herself so that she isn't a foregone conclusion. We'll talk more about this in the next section. She also continues to subtly seduce me in the ways she dresses, acts and communicates.

I love to dress sexy for my husband. I pay attention to what he likes and incorporate that into my daily style and especially on date night.

I see so many women dress up for their boyfriends but not their husbands. It's easy, on Friday night, to differentiate between those who are courting from those who have tied the knot. Of course there are exceptions, but as a general rule, we stop dolling ourselves up. We can't stop being the person that the man of our dreams will be attracted to.

I pursue Kimberly as if she's a prize worth having. The magic in this is that when you value something so highly that you go after it with fervor, the object of your desire becomes enhanced in your eyes. When you continue to pursue something as if it were a prize, its value grows rather than diminishes over time, just as Mihaly stated.

"When you continue to pursue something as if it were a prize, its value grows rather than diminishes over time..."

The cool part is that not only does your mate maintain a high esteem in your eyes, but your esteem for them enhances their esteem for themselves. When they feel worthy of pursuit, it supports the mindset and behaviors they engaged in at the beginning to attract and magnetize you to them. In other words, by acting as if they are worthy, they become worthy. And when they feel worthy, they will behave as though worthy of pursuing. If you both have this mindset, real magic will happen. Romance is about falling in love. In the context of marriage, it's about falling in love over and over again.

The movie *50 First Dates* with Adam Sandler (Henry) and Drew Barrymore (Lucy) was an extreme and comical example of the tact we need to have with our mates. In case

"Romance is about falling in love. In the context of marriage, it's about falling in love over and over again."

you haven't seen the movie, Lucy lost her capacity for long-term memory in a car accident. Every morning when she wakes up, she has no memory of the day before. Enter the character Henry, played by Adam Sandler, who falls in love with Lucy after fortuitously meeting her in an oceanside café. Henry's challenge, he quickly learns, is that Lucy doesn't remember him from one day to the next. All the romancing and wooing he does on Tuesday doesn't translate to Wednesday. He has to get her to fall in love with him all over again, every single day. Amazingly enough, in the end, he manages to marry her.

The funny and not-so-funny thing about this (guys, I'm talking to you), is that women are very much like this. They tend to wake up every morning having "forgotten" some or almost everything we did up to that point to woo them, make them feel loved and show them how significant they are in our life. In other words, the bank account you've been making deposits into *seems* to miraculously go to a zero balance at midnight, every night.

It doesn't, actually. Everything you've ever done to support your marriage is still saved up in there, kind of like your 401K that gets the obligatory $5,000-18,000 tax-free contribution every year. The 401K gives you security, but it won't give you excitement and passion.

Passion and excitement might be likened more to "playing" the stock market. In the case of day trading, you need focus, intention, specialized skills and a tolerance for risk. You don't buy a stock and forget about it. You watch, listen, learn, make moves and hopefully have fun with it. It's just like that with your marriage.

Now back to the movie. After Henry and Lucy get married, Henry comes up with the brilliant idea of making a short, documentary video of his life with Lucy up to that point. He keeps the video in a player next to the bed with a note that says "Push Play". Every morning when she wakes up, she sees the note, plays the video, and gets a pre-frame into the life she is living with this man. In the movie, it circumvents the daily need for him to explain their relationship to her and get her to fall in love with him all over again. This is a fun story but don't get any ideas. A highlight reel of all your past experiences together won't preclude you from having to court your mate. It is a fun idea though. Wouldn't we all benefit from watching a movie of all our best times together? It would help us focus on what really matters most.

I love the idea of the Stack. Stacking great times you've had together by writing them in your journal reinforces the positive experiences you've shared. In fact, when you write about an event within 24 hours of experiencing it, it's as if you get to relive it in your mind, doubling the positive anchor you have with your mate. I journal about magical moments, thoughtful gestures and sweet things he's whispered in my ear. To stack the positive anchors is a valuable tool to remind you just how great things can be.

Solving the Paradox

Marriage is about security and certainty, however, romance and passion is about uncertainty and excitement. This is the paradox introduced in the previous chapter. In *Mating in Captivity* when Esther Perel asked the question "Can we desire what we already have?" she later answered the question by asking, "What makes you think you *have* that which you desire?" It's an ominous question that's well worth contemplating. By virtue of the fact that up to 67% of all marriages (first, second and third marriages combined) end in divorce, that which people think they "have" is but an illusion. Don't forget that, of those that remain married, only some fraction of them have what anyone would describe as an inspiring marriage. Once again, I don't tell you these things to scare you, I tell you to wake you out of complacency.

"Marriage is about security and certainty, however, romance and passion is about uncertainty, variety and excitement."

Remember, desire and attraction are born in the "space" between two polar opposites. The implication of there being a pursuer and a pursuee is that there is a "space" between you that you are dying to close. As soon as someone believes they have the object of their desire, the space is gone. The pursuit is finished. The game is over. Once the object of desire is had, the desire for it wanes. In other words, once you get what you are pursuing, you stop pursuing it.

The irony in all this is that once you stop pursuing it, you don't really have it anymore. Because if you stop the chase, the value of the person diminishes in your eyes (mind and heart), and when their value diminishes, you treat them accordingly and then they feel less valued. And when they feel less valued by you, if you don't turn things around, you won't have them anymore.

The concept of pursuit is a component of almost every ambition you can think of. Whether building a business, learning to fly an airplane, growing a garden, or building a muscular physique. Once you get what you want, if you don't keep doing what you did to get it, it will go away. And even then, what you did to get where you are often isn't good enough to get you where you want to go or even maintain what you have. That's why complacency and mediocrity are so scary.

If we are to reconcile this conundrum of having needs for both love *and* passion, certainty *and* variety, security *and* excitement; we need to first realize that we have most likely confused *love* with *merging*.

It's easy to understand why we have done this. After all, marriage is all about becoming ONE, right? The Bible talks about two becoming one flesh. Marrying couples often use the metaphor of using two candles to light one "unity" candle to symbolize this. This oneness means many things including sexual union and the sharing of one's heart, soul, and life together. It implies a merging of many things but it does not, or at least should not, imply a merging of self. When I say self, I mean that part of you that makes you uniquely you. That part of you that makes you separate from your mate—your unique fingerprint, voice, purpose, perspective or vision. The part of you that was uniquely you, is uniquely you, and will always be uniquely you as you grow in your own fullness.

When you continue to grow your SELF upwards in your true potential, the polarizing "space" between you and your mate that results from that will magnetize you to each other. That's what the next section is about—the final element to having a life-long, passionate love affair that most people only dream about. But first, we need to talk a little about sex…

ACTION STEPS

1. Start pursuing your mate as if they are a prize worth having.
2. Remember that there is certainty in love, but it is uncertainty, variety and mystery that fuel passion. Think about how you might spice things up by consistently introducing a little healthy variety and mystery into your relationship.
3. If you wanted to, what would you do to make your mate fall in love with you all over again? How would you dress? How would you conduct yourself? How would you communicate with them? What would you do differently than you are doing now?

SEXXX
(WHY YOU NEED TO BE
HAVING IT)

Every true lover knows that the moment of greatest satisfaction comes when ecstasy is long over. And he beholds before him the flower which has blossomed beneath his touch.

—Don Juan DeMarco

REALLY? DO WE REALLY need coaching on sex? After all, we live in the age of enlightenment. Or do we? We actually live in the information age. It's not the same thing.

Let me enlighten you about something. If you don't regularly describe your sex life using words like "amazing", "spiritual", "indescribable", or "mind-altering", then you probably need to read this chapter. If your sexual experiences don't consistently leave you wondering why you don't do it more often, one or all of 3 things are getting in the way.

First, you may have disempowering beliefs (myths) about sex; second, you may not realize the profound importance of sex in your marriage; and third, you may not actually know what you are doing. That said, technique actually has very little to do with the quality of one's sexual experience. The most profound and enjoyable experiences happen not because one knows where to stroke, with how many strokes and with how much pressure. They happen spontaneously when one or both partners are in the right *space* in their minds or rather "out of their minds" and in their hearts.

In the context of marriage, sex is one of the most polarizing things a couple can do. What could be more polarizing than a penis and a vagina, male energy vs. female energy, or the engagement of a ravisher and a ravishee? Nothing exemplifies, supports and reinforces the polarity in a marriage more than playful, passionate sex.

However, if this is true, why are so many couples experiencing dispassionate and often sexless marriages? Why does love not necessarily equal desire?

"In the context of marriage, sex is one of the most polarizing things a couple can do.

And, how do you maintain attraction and desire in a long-term relationship? These are the questions we want to answer here and in the remaining chapters. We crave to desire and be desired.

We want to want and be wanted. And if you desire the one you are with, well, life is really good. So let's get down and dirty by first dispelling some commonly-held myths about sex that can stymie your potential for a fulfilling sexual relationship and marriage.

Dispelling Myths about Sex

Myths may be the wrong word to use in this context. They are really beliefs that may govern or influence the quality of your connection with your mate, the quality and frequency of sex—and they can ultimately screw up your life. Myths, in this context, are things we might believe to be true that are, in fact, detrimental to a healthy relationship and a healthy sexuality. It is my hope that if any of these are a part of your experience, you will at least entertain an alternative perspective, and allow yourself the gift of new possibilities.

Myth #1 – A great relationship has nothing to do with sex.

True, if you're not married! A primary difference between a good friendship and a good marriage is sex. You don't need sex to be great friends. However, you must have sex, if not great sex, to have a great marriage.

Dr. Phil McGraw in his #1 bestseller, *Relationship Rescue*, suggests that sex provides couples a respite from the rat race, a place they can go to relax, reconnect, and stay involved. He also adds that without sex your relationship is reduced to "one devoid of uniqueness."

Marriages with unsatisfying sex are more often than not on the road to alienation, infidelity and divorce. Extramarital affairs happen not necessarily because of lack of love, but often because of the absence of sex or, more poignantly, gratifying sex. Individuals going outside their marriage for sex usually aren't looking for love; rather they are looking to gratify an unmet need. That need often takes form in the excitement and eroticism of being with someone who desires them and allows them to be sexually open without being judged.

Good sex is an integral part of a healthy marriage. A great marriage depends on an open, loving and expanding sexual connection. Sex is a continual validation of the commitment made at the altar. It is an act of honoring your mate. It's a testimony that says "today, I have once again chosen you." Sex is not optional. In fact, the Bible refers to it as "due benevolence."

First Corinthians 7:3-5 says:

> Let the husband render to his wife due benevolence: and likewise also the wife to the husband. The wife hath not power of her own body, but the husband: and likewise also the husband hath not power of his own body, but the wife. Defraud ye not one the other, except it be with consent for a time, that ye may give yourselves to fasting and prayer; and come together again, that Satan tempts you not for your incontinency.

Sexual intimacy is a "conjugal duty" in a marriage. This suggests that it is not optional. To deprive or deny your spouse of sexual fulfillment is to defraud them (biblically speaking). In other words, it's a breach of contract. When you got married, you promised each other that you would meet each other's needs, and that your mate would not have to go anywhere else to have them met. It was not a conditional promise.

That said, sex isn't to be generally treated as an exchange either. Although this is how it has been treated for thousands of years, we have socially evolved to a higher place. Just about every marriage book out there teaches a model that essentially views sex as a commodity to be bargained for as it has been over the ages. They teach things like the way to a man's heart is through his penis, and the way to a woman's vagina is through her heart. They reduce sex to a biological need to be satisfied much like the need for eating and sleeping. However, if that's how you treat it, your sex life will be reduced to a simple meat and potatoes diet. Macaroni and cheese hastily prepared from a box will satisfy your hunger, but it will never give you the joy of a gourmet meal prepared with love and artistry. And it certainly won't keep you from wanting to eat out. While there is a time for meeting each other's sexual needs just for the sake of it, doing so for that reason only, significantly limits our potential for a passionate and sexually gratifying marriage.

Myth #2 – Great sex just doesn't happen in a monogamous relationship.

Not true! However, it's a rare experience. You know, sort of like seeing a comet or a lunar eclipse. It happens, just uncommonly. Why? Because we allow the minutia of our lives to distract us from what is really important. We stop treating our lover like a lover and everything goes to hell in a hand basket from there.

It's also common for a committed couple to lose sexual desire for each other. This is a phenomenon that happens due to a loss of polarity and/or lack of consistent personal growth. Learning to nurture and grow the attraction, desire and passion within a committed relationship is what this book is all about, so stay with me.

Great sex outside a committed relationship is an *event*. Great sex within a committed relationship is an *experience* that begins long before the act of sex, and perpetuates long after. The alchemic interplay of love, romance and sex when cultivated in a monogamous relationship is kind of like getting to have all the cake and ice cream you want, albeit possibly gluten and dairy free.

Myth #3 – Sex is for procreation only.

This is for the rare puritan reading this book out of curiosity. Sex is a gift given us by God. Sex, along with the power of choice, and the ability to bring meaning to our lives, are what separate us from the animal kingdom. Putting these 3 together, we as human beings have the ability to choose to have meaningful sex. If it were only for procreation, God would not have given us desire, nor would she have made it pleasurable. For further study, see the appendix for additional materials on the role that religion has taken in robbing people of their *God-given* gift of sexuality.

Myth #4 – Men want sex more than women (or men are the more "high-desire" partner).

This is a myth perpetuated by social pressure and the fact that both men and women, have generally never felt comfortable expressing their true needs, desires and problems because of that social pressure. Speaking in generalizations of course, if a man has low libido, he feels less "manly." His lack of sexual desire is a blow to his masculinity and not something he will readily admit, take responsibility for, seek help for, and certainly not share in a questionnaire. If a woman has a high sex drive and finds her needs consistently not being met, she's conditioned to keep her mouth shut. In high school, the high-desire girls were always "sluts." They're told that "guys are the ones that think about nothing but sex."

Forget every preconception you may have. Every relationship has a high-desire and a low-desire partner, and it's not gender determined. The high-desire partner in one relationship could be the low-desire partner in the next.

Even more interestingly, the "low-desire" partner is often really the higher-desire partner masquerading as a person disinterested in sex. They often wear a "low-desire" mask because they are emotionally turned off by their mate or are dissuaded from having sex with them due to their clumsy and uninspiring nature.

Myth #5 – Sex is "dirty" or immoral.

You're darn right it's "dirty"! If it's done right, that is. Woody Allen says, "Sex is dirty, that's why you should save it for someone you love!" Well, in the context of swapping bodily fluids, I think he's right. So why do we have this myth? I think it ties in with Myth #3. The belief that sex is "dirty" from a philosophical standpoint is an indoctrination that some people have had instilled and perpetuated by their religion, their parents, their education and social influences. It's an indoctrination just like the belief that money is the root of all evil, you should never talk to strangers, or you must go to college to succeed in life. These things are treated as absolute truths and influence our decision making and how we interpret the world around us.

The belief that sex is "dirty" has been perpetuated by fear rather than love. A parent's fear of a daughter getting pregnant. A husband's fear of a wife's overt sexuality. A church's fear of losing control over its members. Many churches use guilt to control their members by keeping them in a perpetual cycle of sin-guilt-repentance. Associating sex with sin and sin with guilt has made sex a "dirty" word. Certainly there is "dirty" sex, in the sinful sense of it, such as sex performed for money, sex that degrades human beings, sex that is used to control another, and sex that is manipulative. In an effort to prevent teen girls from doing something stupid, parents may say, "If you have sex before you're married, no decent guy is going to want you." The message they get is that sex makes them unclean. What a travesty!

If you have moral hang-ups (religious beliefs) about sex or specific sexual practices that are barriers to a fulfilling sex life with your lover, please see the appendix for additional reading material on the subject. What if your beliefs about sexual immorality were based not on the Bible but on religious and social tradition? What if you learned that it is actually God's design for a husband and wife to experience each other's bodies without limits?

An all-you-can-eat buffet of sex between 2 consenting adults who love each other is one of the most beautiful things in the world along with a baby being born, a desert sunset, and seeing 2 people in love. I believe, whether it's "dirty" or not (morally and philosophically), is in the mutual intention of the 2 consenting adults doing it.

Myth #6 – All men ever want is sex! It's the only thing on their minds.

This statement is false when men are in a mutually loving and engaging relationship. However, it is oftentimes very true when a marriage is cold, stale and dispassionate, and they're not "getting any." In other words, guys only obsess about sex when they aren't having enough of it. Otherwise, they're thinking about cars, football, golf, fishing, making money, and, oh yeah baby... how blessed we are to have YOU in our lives. Something to think about.

Myth #7 – Intimacy increases desire.

Not necessarily. Intimacy and passion are 2 different things. Intimacy and sensuality are 2 different things. Intimacy and sex are 2 different things. Intimacy does not beget desire. Intimacy begets connection, comfort, familiarity and security. Intimacy is the experience of loving, sharing, knowing and accepting. Intimacy can lead to the kind of sex one engages in to foster connection, reassurance, and love – all good things, but not desire. Not *desire* in the sensual, erotic sense as in "I want you!" You know, the kind of desire where you both start tearing your clothes off the second you see each other.

Sensual desire comes from liking what you see, being intrigued by what you see, being curious about what you don't see, and wanting a peek behind the curtain.

The intrigue is cultivated through expansion in your human capacity; growing and evolving yourself as a human being so you're not a foregone conclusion. Make an effort to keep it fresh and fun. Maybe take a belly dance class, read a few books on how to be a better lover, and be willing to try new things together. When your engagement is a little bit unpredictable; it raises the excitement level exponentially.

Make an effort to not replay a prior experience but to make each one a unique encounter.

It comes from getting a couple of licks of chocolate ice cream and wanting more. Desire forms in the gap between what you take for granted and what is intangible.

It's disappointing that we often to have a life-altering experience before we realize what's most important. Sometimes we have to lose the very thing we love the most before we realize how much it meant to us. Spend some time thinking about how it would feel if your mate disappeared from your life. If you can get into this space, it will shake you from complacency and eliminate you taking each other for granted.

In other words, desire is the emotion you experience when you long for what you don't have, whereas intimacy comes from being secure in what you do have. The secret to desire is not intimacy, but rather maintaining your mystery, intrigue, and sense of self through consistent personal development.

Once you have a taste of intense desire for your mate, you'll never want that feeling to go away. When you incorporate polarization and differentiation into the equation your desire will increase. These elements act like a catalyst, similar to yeast rising your dough.

***Myth #8 –* You both need to "be in the mood" to have sex.**

Another way of putting this is that all the planets need to be in alignment before sex can, or should, happen. This is one of the most destructive and sabotaging beliefs you can have. Modern marriages are fraught with challenges that couples didn't have in our parent's and grandparent's day. If the pressures of careers, child rearing and finances aren't enough to quell sexual desire; then the inherent depolarizing of men and women in egalitarian marriages is sure to do the trick. If anything, you need to be having more sex for all the reasons listed later in this chapter.

***Myth #9 –* Your sexual prime is in your 20's and 30's.**

This is biologically true but not experientially true. The reason for this is that there is a direct correlation between one's ability to have passionate sex and their level of personal development. This is why most people don't have "golden" sex until their golden years. It often takes decades of personal growth to get to the place where one has the maturity and authenticity to have truly intimate sex.

Reasons Why You Need Sex in Your Marriage

Do you need a reason to have sex? Well, there are more reasons than you've probably guessed why you *need* sex in your life. What if you found out that your marriage depended on it? What if you found out that your health depended on it? As people mature in their relationships and get older, often out of ignorance they take for granted the role that sex plays in a healthy life.

A primary reason this happens is a natural diminishing sexual desire. I don't think its news to anyone that as we get older our desire for sex goes down. Does that mean that sex also diminishes in importance with age? Absolutely not! Does your appetite for food diminish with age? For some it does. Do you stop eating just because you aren't hungry? No way. You eat for energy, nutrition, variety and pleasure.

Likewise, as you mature, sex serves as a multi-functional activity to add variety, connection, devotion and recreation to you relationship. You don't do it so much anymore because you desire sex. You do it because you desire that person and want to expand your experience with them. You are about to see just what a key role sex plays in maintaining your emotional, mental and physical wellbeing.

Reason #1 – **Procreation**

Okay, this is obviously optional. However, it is difficult for 2 committed people in love not to want to make babies.

Reason #2 – **Connection**

The physical intimacy of sex uniquely connects you to your mate. This crazy world we live in with work, kids, schedules, household duties, and so forth all work to disconnect us from our lover. Making love is a great way to reconnect, reassure, and reaffirm the promises made in the beginning. Maybe, just maybe, if couples had more sex they would feel more connected instead of waiting to feel more connected to have sex.

Reason #3 – **Bonding**

The intimate physical connection that comes through sexual intercourse bonds 2 people together as lovers, and mitigates the propensity to look outside the relationship for fulfillment. The meeting of each other's sexual needs fulfills the pledge made at the altar. Marriage is the "act of uniting" as one. Sex is the physical declaration and affirmation of that.

Reason #4 – **Demonstration of love**

Both men and women can use sex as a way to demonstrate their love and affection. It's a way of saying, "Baby, I love you and I don't want there to be any physical space between us." "I want to make you feel good." "I want to give you pleasure." "I want you to know that you are the special person in my life." Sex is an active demonstration of commitment and surrender to each other. It's a gift of love to our mate and to ourselves.

Reason #5 – **Act of devotion**

In a marriage, sex is a primary way to demonstrate to our mate that we are theirs. It's an offering of ourselves that affirms the vows we took at the altar to give ourselves only to our beloved. In Tantra, this is known as divine union.

Don't underestimate the power of The Devotion as we like to call it. The Devotion is a weekly, if not daily, gift that we give each other. It ensures that we connect on an emotional and physical level (without any grandiose expectations) for a few minutes before we go to sleep each night. Many times one of us is tired or mentally exhausted and not up for making love. However, the low-desire partner will almost always be happily willing to devote. It is relaxing and enjoyable; not vigorous; nor a commitment to fully engaged sex. It's an affirmation to each other that they mean the most to you and that you are not ignoring their needs. Often though, it turns into much more than that. This ties directly into Myth #8.

Reason #6 – Rejuvenation

Sex is good for the wellbeing of your marriage. It makes you feel good. It releases endorphins into your bloodstream. Sex can also feel cleansing by releasing pent-up energy and anxiety. As one husband aptly put it, "Sex gets the poison out."

Reason #7 – Recreation

Sex is fun, or at least it should be. Couples that have fun together stay together. Your bodies are like an endless playground of possibilities. Doesn't humping like rabbits sound more fun than going to the movies? Who says they have to be mutually exclusive?

Reason #8 – Reset

Making love is a great way to periodically (daily, weekly, monthly) "reset" your relationship. Your coming together (no pun intended) in the bedroom is an expression and validation of every other reason listed here. It says, "I love you." "We are good." "Everything is okay," "I'm here for you." "You are still my special one." "I choose you." etc.

Reason #9 – Self-expression

Sex is an opportunity for individuals to take off the mask they wear in public and express the side of themselves that they suppress because of social norms. Social pressure, politics and religious dogma all make it unacceptable for some people to be true to themselves. Proper gender roles as mandated by society have precluded men, and more often women, from expressing their true sexuality overtly. Behind-closed-doors sex often provides people a canvas for self-expression and release. Sexuality, as with most things, can be expressed as an art form, as exemplified in the *Kama Sutra*.

Sometimes you might feel like who you or your lover are in the bedroom is incongruent with who you are in your public life. Not necessarily true. We all have many facets to our personalities. For every need to be harnessed there is an opposite need to be unleashed. For every need to be in control, we have the need to be wild. For every need for structure, we have the complementary need for spontaneity. And for those tending toward the prudish or puritanical, there might just be a little Pamela Anderson or Tommy Lee dying to express themselves.

Reason # 10 – **Longevity**

Studies have shown that a happy marriage and a prolonged sex life are key to longevity. People in love have higher levels of endorphins, and lower levels of destructive lactic acid and cortisol. The challenges and strains of life are more easily endured with a mate to share their experiences with. Being loved releases oxytocin, known to reduce blood pressure. But more to the point, sex is a huge stress reliever and can factor significantly in the prevention of heart disease. Men also have a built-in need to ejaculate. A man's prostate produces semen most, if not all, of his life. If your prostate is producing semen, the semen needs to be regularly expelled and regenerated for the health of the prostate. Many doctors have concluded that prostate cancer could be largely mitigated by maintaining an active sex life into old age. The axiom "use it or lose it" holds true once again.

Reason #11 – **Polarity**

Repeating myself from the opening page of this chapter, sex is one of the most polarizing things a couple can do. What could be more polarizing than a penis and a vagina, male energy vs. female energy, or the engagement of a ravisher and a ravishee? Nothing exemplifies, supports and reinforces the polarity in a marriage more than playful, passionate sex.

Reason #12 – Variety

One of our fundamental human needs is for variety. Sexual connection and exploration is a wonderful way to add and maintain variety in your relationship and your life. As I alluded at the beginning of this section, as adults enter their true sexual prime, sex is less about filling a physical need as it is about experiencing and connecting with your mate in new and exciting ways, that inspire and facilitate personal and spiritual growth, and adventure. Now that's variety!

Reason #13 – Personal development

It's been often said that a couple's sex life is a window into the health of the relationship. This is because sex (good or bad, frequent or never) is a by-product or fruit of the health, wellbeing and evolution of the 2 people in the relationship. Good sex is often a symptom of a "good" working relationship. Transcendental sex is often a marker of being on a path of emotional and spiritual evolution. Any emotional barriers or hang-ups one might have to being able to let oneself go (in a sexual context), be fully present and relinquish their ego, are a signal for personal growth.

Reason #14 – Sex is a great pain reliever

We are all too familiar with the cliché, "Not tonight honey, I have a headache." The funny thing about this is that sex is an amazing cure for a headache. We happen to know this from personal experience.

Reason #15 – You're horny and can't contain yourselves

You know how it is when you are tearing each other's clothes off in a fit of passion…right? Or does that only happen in the movies? I sincerely hope not. I'm talking about spontaneous "I want you right here and now" sex. No plan, no agenda, just unbridled primitive sex.

So there it is. We've busted some myths about sex, and given you all the reasons you need to be having sex. All that brings me to these compelling questions. As enamored with sex as the world is, why do we have so many issues with it? Why do couples struggle so much with sexual fulfillment? Why do we often lose desire for each other, and what do we need to do to keep the passion alive?

Notable sex therapist, Dr. David Schnarch, answered these questions when he posed the idea that people have sex [only] up to the level of their personal development. What on earth is he talking about? Well, once again we are confronted with the idea that things can be good right up to the point where they aren't. In the context of passion and sex, what used to work, or what excited and inspired you in the beginning no longer works. This isn't because you've developed unrealistic expectations or just need a stronger drug. It's because humans have an innate need for a meaningful, fulfilling and inspiring life experience. And the only way for us to have this experience is to have constant and never-ending growth.

It's understandable how in the beginning, a person might be patient and understanding of a lover who is uncertain and tentative about their sexuality. However, if 10 years later they have not advanced, developed and grown in this area, frustration and discontent is likely to manifest. Any area of your life that doesn't become more complex as a result of personal evolution will eventually stagnate and die. Most couple's sex lives are made up of leftovers. When you take everything that she won't do and add it to everything he won't do, what's left over is their sex life. The objective in your own sex life might be to shift things so that there are no leftovers.

Sex is about connecting with your partner's heart, mind and soul, not their genitals. The ability to experience passion is one of the things that separate us from the animals. In the context of marriage, passion isn't about having an intense desire and love for sex. It's about having a sensationally intense wanting and desire for a specific person, your mate. It's wanting *them,* and to have sex with *them.* When you want each other, foreplay isn't really a part of sex. It's more the interplay that goes on between you when you're not even thinking of having sex.

"When you take everything that she won't do and add it to everything he won't do, what's left over is their sex life."

When you really want each other, sex is no longer about touching each other's bodies as it is about touching each other's minds. For this to be the case, each of us must be the person that is *capable* of touching our mate's minds, hearts and souls. To do this requires consistent, multi-faceted personal development.

ACTION STEPS

1. Get honest with yourself and identify what (if any) beliefs you might have about sex that could be preventing you from consistently connecting with your mate in a meaningful way, meeting your mate's needs at a high level, or even allowing you to express yourself authentically.

2. Consider confiding in your mate what these beliefs are and how you would appreciate their patience and understanding as you work together to explore expanded definitions of what a healthy sex life looks like.

3. Of all the reasons to have more sex, which ones seem difficult for you to grasp or embrace, and could these be the springboard for your own personal development?

4. Consider using sex as a mechanism for fulfilling more of your emotional needs as a couple. It isn't the product or sum of a mathematical equation. It's a key coefficient (constant) within the equation.

5. Remember, sex in a passionate marriage isn't about relieving oneself of an urge. Rather, it's an expression of desire, wanting, and commitment to one person.

SECTION 3:
PERSONAL
DEVELOPMENT

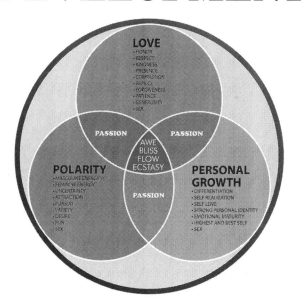

TRUE NOBILITY—
BEING YOUR BEST

There is nothing noble in being superior to your fellow man; true nobility is being superior to your former self.

—Ernest Hemingway

THERE'S A RESTAURANT IN Tokyo called Les Creations de Narisawa. There are 4 words or phrases that come to my mind to describe the food preparations by Chef Yoshihiro Narisawa: impeccable, artistic, mind blowing and paradigm shifting. Imagine a slab of freshly sawn wood, covered in what appears to be grainy earth, moss, stones and forest foliage all of which are edible. A hollowed branch holds a swallow of fresh water taken from a spring-fed mountain stream while sounds of rainforest wildlife are piped in through a hidden speaker hidden within the delectable menagerie. The excellence exemplified by Chef Narisawa is inspiring to say the least! It compels you to raise your standards and live your life to a higher level. What would it be like if we could use words like impeccable, artistic and inspiring to describe our own pursuits? What about our marriage?

The world is enamored with excellence. We admire, envy, and even worship peak performers who tap into, harness, and exemplify what to most seem like the outer reaches of human potential. We are entranced by the talent and performances of the likes of Laird Hamilton, Michael Jordan, Tiger Woods, Wayne Gretzky, Michael Phelps, Roger Federer, Serena Williams, Michael Jackson, Andrea Bocelli, Al Pacino, Meryl Streep, David Copperfield, Massimo Bottura, and the Monets and Rembrandts of the world. We love hearing about a daredevil rock climber making a solo ascent up an "impossible" rock face; or reading about the newest 25-year-old tech billionaire who's changed the way we communicate with each other forever.

Some of us are inspired by these individuals to aspire to our own greatness.

But for some reason, most of us are content to experience excellence vicariously. We tend to be experts at viewing sports and spewing related statistics, watching movies, listening to music, using a microwave, eating, drinking, playing video games, gossiping, arguing, and avoiding things that rub us the wrong way. We think that "excellence" is the birthright of a select chosen few who are born with the right genetics or into the right family. The truth is that we are often unaware of what we are capable of, we don't honor our potential, and we succumb to sheer laziness because we don't grasp the benefits of pursuing our own excellence. We forsake our birthright. This is something I hope to help change.

"That's just the way I am" Syndrome

The media has actually done us an enormous disservice. It has taken an extremely small percentage (less than 1%) of the population who have outstanding accomplishments and put them right in our faces. When we look in the mirror, we are expecting (hoping) to see these extraordinary individuals in our reflection somehow. And when we don't, we are either discouraged, apathetic or dissuaded from being the best that we can be because the standard seems unattainable. So we write off our true potential not realizing that as Hemmingway said, the "true nobility is being superior to your former self" not in trying to be someone or something that you aren't.

That said, how often do you hear someone say in response to a judgment or criticism, "Well, that's just the way I am!" or "If you really loved me, you would love me just the way I am." I think we *should* love our mates just the way they are. I think we should love ourselves just the way we are. However, that doesn't excuse them or us from growing up from who and what we are, to what we are truly capable of. I think by now you get the message that positive movement, growth and evolution are a critical component of experiencing reward, fulfillment and passion not only in your marriage but in your life.

In his book, *Reinventing the Body, Resurrecting the Soul,* Deepak Chopra suggests that we are not bound by the dictates of our DNA but rather that we have the ability to switch on or off its programming through conscious intention. Mihaly Csikszentmihalyi corroborates this idea in his book *Flow* when he says, "…consciousness has developed the ability to override its genetic instructions and to set its own course of action." I tend to believe them. So, don't succumb to "That's just the way I am" syndrome.

People say things to me all the time like, "I'm just not comfortable doing _____ in the bedroom", or "I am just not an adventurous person", or "I am just naturally impatient", or "I'm not a good cook", or "I'm not the athletic type", or "I'm just naturally not affectionate", or "I'm just the jealous type", or "I have diabetes because it runs in my family". They use these "just the way I am" statements to rationalize not growing beyond what they are comfortable doing. I catch myself doing it too!

The problem with this mentality is that it causes us to get stuck. Instead of growing upward toward our true potential, we mire ourselves at a level of development that doesn't serve our relationship or us. Can you imagine what it would be like if we all stopped emotionally growing when we were 5 years old? To say to yourself or anyone else, "That's just the way I am" would be like a 5-year-old saying, "Well, that's just the way I am" after throwing a tantrum for not getting her way. That may well be "just the way they are" at 5 years old but I think we can all agree that it is a behavior that is beneficial to outgrow and one we are expected to outgrow. If we stayed emotional 5-year-olds, we would all be throwing tantrums and lying through our teeth to get our way.

At what point are we to stop growing and evolving ourselves as human beings? When we are 5? 12? 18? 27? 60? What areas of our lives should be exempt from growth and improvement? Our cooking? Our fitness? Our sexuality? Our capacity to love? Our spiritual reference? The answer to the first question is that we often stop growing when we reach a level that supports the minimal quality of life that we are willing to endure. Sounds pretty pathetic, doesn't it? Well that's what happens.

We tend to learn and develop ourselves to the degree that we need to just get by, at least in certain areas where we are uncomfortable growing. Most people are very mediocre parents, lovers, cooks, drivers, computer users, stewards of their bodies and spiritual seekers. They stagnate at the level where things work just well enough to give them a minimal level of comfort and/or certainty. Besides being unfulfilling, the problem with settling for this kind of existence is that it gets you by right up to the point when it doesn't. The point when it doesn't is the point when your marriage is falling apart, your kids are getting into trouble, your job is in jeopardy, you're chronically unhappy or you're diagnosed with a major health problem.

Unfortunately, it's often only in the presence of necessity or painful feedback that we're motivated to grow, make a change, or do things differently. This wake-up call can be a launching point for a new and improved you in any area of your life.

I periodically take account of areas in my life that have been on autopilot for years and ask myself how I can make them better, more efficient or completely different.

This can be with your cooking, computer skills, exercise, communication, or teaching your child a new skill, just to name a few. I'm often amazed at how this can intensify the gratification of even the most menial task.

Paradoxically, the areas that are the most uncomfortable for us to improve on are the areas that often most need our attention. They are also the areas that will most dramatically improve the quality of your life.

Just getting by isn't going to get you where you want to go. Being the best that you can be is about raising your standards and pushing beyond your self-imposed

"Paradoxically, the areas that are the most uncomfortable for us to improve on are the areas that often most need our attention."

limitations. Don't fall victim to "That's just the way I am" syndrome. If I did that when I was a child, I'd still be walking pigeon toed and wearing leg braces. When I was 6 years old, I had a condition that caused my feet to "naturally" turn in. My mom lovingly encouraged me to practice walking with my feet straight ahead. So I practiced and practiced and practiced until walking straight was "just the way I was". Was I denying something I was, to become something I wasn't? Absolutely not! I was growing myself into my true potential. What if when we were 14 months old and our parents were encouraging us to walk we said, "No Dada, I'm not a walker, I'm a crawler. Never been a walker. I'm a born crawler. In fact, I'm just going to stick with crawling and sucking on mommy's tits for the rest of my life because that's who I am." Do you know anyone like that? I'll tell you what, learning to walk isn't easy and neither is getting weaned off the tit. Growing up is a life-long process and if you think you've arrived, truth be told, you're probably at least a bit delusional.

Walmart Syndrome

I'm not a big fan of Walmart on many levels. I rarely shop at Walmart and when I do, it's not without reluctance. Here's an example of why. A year or so ago, my wife bought about $400 worth of "domestic necessities" from Walmart to outfit a new house we were moving into. After sorting through all the toiletries, kitchen utensils and cleaning supplies, she assembled a small bag of items she decided she did not want. So she recruited me to go to Walmart to return the unwanted items for a refund. Out of deep love for my wife, I drove the 30 minutes to the nearest Walmart, stood in line for 30 minutes, got $30 worth of refunds and drove the 30 minutes back home. All in all, the trip took me approximately an hour and a half. That's 1 hour and 30 minutes, plus $7 worth of gas. If my time was worth even $15/hour, I just might have broken even.

But that's not the worst part. The big rub was how demoralizing it was to stand in line at Walmart. I mean no judgment on the poor, despondent and unsophisticated people I observed, because there *I* was standing in line amongst them. Maybe I was one of them! For all I know, *you* might have purchased this book at Walmart if I was fortunate enough to get it on their shelves. That said, my observation was that the average Walmart shopper is trying to get the mostest for the leastest; the leastest amount of money and the leastest amount of effort. And in the process, they are cheating themselves of good health and wellbeing. I mean, where else can you go (Costco aside) and fill up an oversized shopping cart with "food" for $100 and do it while riding around in a store-provided electric scooter? If your average Walmart shopper is representative of a typical American, we are in trouble. I would have to say that 50-75% of all the shoppers I have superficially observed in these stores are suffering from either diabetes, obesity, heart disease, lung cancer, organ failure or some kind or depression. This I'm guessing is largely out of ignorance, partly out of lack of resources, partly out of apathy and somewhat out of laziness.

Oh, I almost forgot the sort-of-funny part about the whole thing that further reinforced my "affection" for Walmart. When Kimberly first made the $400 shopping cart purchase, she stopped for 2 minutes on the way out to treat our daughter to a 50 cent ride on a mechanical horse. Alas, while her attention was momentarily diverted, someone stole the entire shopping cart!

Anyway, this all made me wonder, "Where might I have Walmart syndrome in my own life?" "What areas of my life have I settled for less than my potential because I've taken the path of least resistance?" This inspired me to ask new questions to help me identify if I am working at being the best that I can be, and not just in the obvious areas, but also where I might have blind spots; areas that might be off my radar.

An analogy for these blind spots surfaced recently when I started working with a really talented physical therapist and strength trainer. It quickly became apparent that I was in very poor physical condition. For me this was a big blow since I've been active all my life with cycling, tennis, hiking, physical labor and occasional gym time. However, through all this I've also suffered with chronic back and joint pain, as well as tendonitis from multiple injuries. What I soon discovered was that I've spent my life, by default, reinforcing (favoring) my natural strengths or tendencies and ignoring (neglecting) my weaknesses. In other words, I have inadvertently developed physical blind spots—areas of weakness that have set me up for consistent physical failure. I learned that when I have used my body in day-to-day life as well as in the gym, I had learned to compensate for areas of weakness by inappropriately overusing areas of perceived strength. The result was a body out of balance with some atrophied muscle groups and other overdeveloped muscle groups. The solution has been to train muscles groups that are very uncomfortable.

The moral is that what we often need to do to take our experience to a new level is the very thing we find most uncomfortable and tend to avoid. The areas of our life that we often make off limits to change or improvement are the very areas that will have the most dramatic impact on the quality of our health, wellbeing and relationships. For me, bringing my muscle physiology into balance and increased strength will change my life forever. Not only will it prevent future injuries and eliminate most of my tendon and joint pain, but it will increase my general level of health, make me more physically available to my family, make me more attractive to my wife and allow me to give more of myself as a contributor.

I've discovered that, oftentimes, even when we gain new awareness of our blind spots, our ability to work on them and alleviate them is very challenging without a coach. A good coach not only gives you perspective on yourself that you can never get on your own, they can also inspire you to push beyond the imaginary limitations that you often think you have. As much as people talk about or strive today for what is known as mindfulness, if you've been walking the earth with the same stride, sitting in your chair with the same posture, eating your food with the same mannerisms, putting the same shoe on the same foot first, going to the same church, hanging out with the same friends, looking at the world and yourself through the same glasses, and you've been doing this for decades; a passing moment of "mindfulness" may possibly bring to your attention your own habitual and ingrained routines, habits, tendencies or nuances that could use improvement. It's curious how often we glimpse a new perspective or awareness of ourselves and then almost instantly forget or disregard it like it never happened. Mindfulness is the state of being conscious or aware of something. But what service does it have for us if we don't act on it for our own betterment or the betterment of the world we live in? Is it mindful to be aware of the global benefits of recycling if we don't make the conscious choice to recycle?

So, here are a few hypothetical, self-analysis type questions to get your eyebrows lifting and your creative juices flowing. These aren't intended to make you dissatisfied with yourself but rather to wake you out of complacency. Because if you're not growing into your true potential, you're not only being unfaithful to yourself, you're being unfaithful to your mate. These questions are significant on multiple levels. First, it's about the reward of being your best YOU that you can be for you. Second, it about the reward of being the best you can be for your mate. And third, it's about being an unfolding mystery that inspires, attracts and magnetizes your mate to you in new, unscripted ways.

Thought-Provoking Questions

1. Are you optimizing your time and skills in your job or career so that you can be home more, and/or realize the most financial gain?
2. Are you expanding yourself through the pursuit of worthwhile personal interests and hobbies?
3. Are you making the most of your time or do you fritter it away in unedifying activities that don't support your goals?

4. We all learned how to walk, but do we walk with the ease and form that will carry us where we want to go through a long life? Or are we actually walking out of balance using the wrong muscles to propel us forward? Ever notice how some people walk and run as if they're floating on air and others look like an unfolding lawn chair?

5. Is our posture representative of the person we want to be, the life we want to live, and the influence we want to have? Maybe what we have been trained to think is good posture, really is bad for your back. Don't take anything for granted.

6. We all know how to breathe, but do we breathe correctly so that we are maintaining a healthy carbon dioxide/oxygen ratio? This may seem strange but our family learned about this from a breathing coach we hired for our daughter.

7. Most of us probably know how to swim but are we dog-paddling our way through life?

8. Does your mate find you desirable and pleasant to look at or do they wonder what happened to the attractive, self-caring person they married?

9. When you communicate with others, do they find your communication style and tone enjoyable or is it annoying, grating and unpleasant?

10. Are you a blabbering gossip or does what you have to say inspire, uplift and encourage people?

11. Do you have good table etiquette or do people find your mannerisms distracting?

12. Is your sexual aptitude growing, developing and evolving, or is it boring, monotonous and uninspiring?

13. Are you growing and evolving spiritually or are you mired in a religious or philosophical box?

14. Does your cooking leave your family and friends saying, "Wow, that was really good!" or would they prefer fast food?

15. Do you know how to cook healthy food that looks and tastes great or are you setting up your family for future health challenges?

Since I consider myself a healthy, gourmet cook, it often surprises me how many people think they eat and cook healthy when they really don't. I have family and friends who are convinced that they eat healthy while filling their shopping carts with processed foods full of sugar and trans fats. And then they blame their obesity or diabetes on genetics. It's a good example of how we can think we're educated or skilled at something but really aren't.

16. Does your skill in the kitchen make meal preparation elegant and fluid or do you struggle to make soup?
17. Are you overweight and out of shape or do you inspire others to a healthier life?
18. Honestly, if you're going to give yourself to your mate as a gift, shouldn't it be perfumed, gift wrapped and thoughtfully selected?
19. Do you inspire your mate to take better care of themselves?
20. Do you have the energy to be effective at work *and* at home or do you lack what it takes to meet the needs of your mate and your family?
21. Most people don't have the energy that they could because of the lifestyle choices they make. Are you eating, drinking, sleeping and exercising in a way that optimizes your energy supply for your mate and your family?
22. Are you developing and sharing your God-given talents?

Your body is the conduit for the expression and sharing of your gifts, your love, and your time. If you don't have your health, it's hard to live and love to your fullest potential. I'm not here to preach at you because as I write this, I can honestly say that I am not being my best in this area. Americans suffer from four maladies that dramatically reduce their overall health and energy levels: stress, poor nutrition, poor sleep and inadequate physical movement. If any, or all, of these things are part of your experience, it's time to start making choices that empower you to be your best for yourself, your mate and your family.

These questions are designed to inspire you out of complacency and leth-argy. You could say, "Well, that's just the way I am" or "They should love me the way I am". You're right, they should. The question is, will they be attracted to you, want you and desire you if you remain the way you are? Will you love yourself?

This reminds me of a story of a woman who was having difficulty getting aroused by her husband after several years of marriage. When they first married, he was rather unskilled and clumsy with regard to his lovemaking, but because she loved him, naturally climaxed easily, and assumed he would improve with time, she wasn't too concerned about it. Fast forward several years and nothing changed except her desire and attraction for him. *Now*, his lack of development as a lover was a source of pain and frustration for her. What worked in the past no longer worked in the present because now she perceived him as selfish, inflexible and unaccommodating. The problem wasn't the fact that one of them changed, but rather that one refused to change.

In his book *In Over Our Heads*, Harvard psychologist Robert Kegan explains how 95% of adults remain frozen in time when it comes to their personal identity and personhood. Once they develop a hard and fast definition of themselves—their sense of who they are—they tend to use that definition as a concrete frame of reference from which to judge, filter and vet all other values, philosophies and paradigms.

As a result, our capacity for empathy, understanding, meaningful growth and "self-transformation" is stunted. Not only are we less capable of expanding ourselves when we do this, it is extremely challenging for us to entertain, embrace and honor another's differences of opinion, values, political leanings or spiritual and philosophical paradigms. We get stuck in a one-dimensional view of the world, of how things are and of how they should be. When this happens, we find ourselves defending those beliefs and values that we think make us "us". And when someone close to us sees the world differently or has a strong difference of opinion, we get riled, upset and defensive. Instead of loving with our heart and soul, we judge, analyze, compare and often condemn with our mind. You can see how this is the perfect set-up for conflict in a marriage. When we are "in our heads", our tendency is to focus on and take issue with those things that don't really matter. Until we learn how to get "out of our minds", our capacity to experience personal growth and marital bliss is limited, if not altogether unavailable. More on this later.

The 3rd Element in the Passionate Marriage Trifecta is Personal Growth. Personal Growth is the secret ingredient to a sustained, passionate, life-long love affair. It's the never-ending process of revealing and realizing your highest and best self. Personal Growth turns you into an unfolding mystery, a blossoming flower and an ever-evolving being. In short, it keeps you feeling alive, looking alive and just plain interesting.

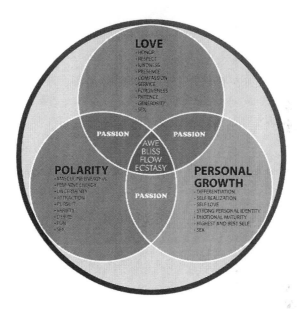

We each have something special and unique inside us to give to the world—a talent, a skill, a message. Developing that gift along with our ability to share it is what really lights us up as human beings. Beholding the phenomenon of this unfolding in your mate is like being the supporting actor in a play where your mate has the leading role. You aren't there to direct them, control them or steal their thunder, but rather to support, appreciate, and cheer them on. Being able to maintain your own sense of self, while unconditionally loving and supporting your mate in being true to themselves, is what really encourages our own evolution in ways that would never happen outside a marriage.

A bonus benefit of you improving you is that it often inspires your mate to improve themselves. This reciprocal interplay can go on throughout your entire life—encouraging each other to be the best they can be.

When you do this for each other and collaboratively with each other, you have the formula for a truly rewarding, fulfilling and inspiring experience.

The key word here is collaboration. So, let's collaborate and explore collaboration a little in the next chapter.

ACTION STEPS

1. If you are honest with yourself, how often have you defended yourself, silently or aloud, with the words "that's just the way I am" in response to a criticism or a request for a change in behavior and perspective?
2. Challenge yourself and formulate a new set of goals for yourself from the "thought-provoking questions" listed earlier in this chapter.
3. Make a list of everything you could do improve or evolve yourself physically, emotionally, intellectually and spiritually. Choose one thing from each category and make a commitment right now to take yourself to a new level as a human being and as a mate. Choose those things that will have the impact of meeting your partner's 7 core needs at a higher level than ever before.

COLLABORATION—THE TANDEM EFFECT

Life is like riding a bicycle. To keep your balance, you must keep moving.
—Albert Einstein

I LOVE THIS QUOTE because it emphasizes the need for movement and forward motion. After all, that's what personal development is all about. That's what marriage is all about. If Einstein had been thinking of marriage when he made this statement, it might have read more like this:

Marriage is like riding a tandem bicycle, in order to enjoy the experience, you've got to love, let go, and collaborate.
—Tad Horning

Individuals in troubled marriages often explain to us how their spouses and them have grown apart over the years and just have nothing in common. We like to tell them that couples don't "grow" apart, they "don't grow" apart. What we mean by that is that it is their lack of growth that is responsible for their condition. In the context of this chapter, it is the lack of *collaborative growth* that's responsible for couples developing an unhealthy space between them. Simply put, growing apart happens when you *fail* to collaborate on your life together.

"Simply put, growing apart happens when you *fail* to collaborate on your life together."

So how in the heck do you get on the same page with your spouse and *stay* on the same page? Well first of all, you've got to define what it means to be on the same page. I think that sometimes we confuse sameness with being in agreement. We're often offended when our mate has different preferences, tastes or beliefs to ours. You just don't need to be on the same page about everything to have a life-long love affair. In fact, you don't want to be. How boring would that be?

Collaboration is working together to expand your relationship and evolve it to new places. Collaboration is supporting each other in the development and realization of our individual talents and life purposes. It's also setting and accomplishing goals that you mutually benefit from. One of the greatest gifts to our marriage has been the choice to invest ourselves in education and personal development together. When we do that, we create a broader and deeper, shared frame of reference that not only gives us a deeper connection, but also provides us a similar set of rules and values that govern our decision making, both as individuals and as a couple. The funny thing is, marriage is inherently a collaboration. I missed this in a previous chapter, but one of our implicit vows is the promise to collaborate together in the creation of a meaningful and fulfilling life. I know that it's an implied vow because, if either one us thought that our fiancé would not collaborate, conspire, and collude with us to have the life we imagine, we would most likely never marry them. Now, all we need to do is to start collaborating with intention.

At an elementary level, collaboration in your marriage means sitting down and saying, "Hey baby, I know we've got a good marriage, but I want a great marriage. I want to take it up a notch. I want to be a better lover and mate, and learn to meet your needs at a higher level. I want our marriage to be the pinnacle experience in our lives. What do you say we go to this passionate marriage weekend I saw advertised?" It is conspiring to go to a *Fly Fishing for Couples* class, yoga retreat, or wine tasting symposium. Maybe it's Salsa dance lessons or training together to compete in your first triathlon.

And it's not always about doing what you *both* want to do. As we'll discover in the next chapter, it's often more about expanding yourself by stepping outside your own boundaries and collaboratively exploring something that juices your mate.

An example of this from the annals of Tad and Kimberly, is Golf. There was a time in my life where I was enamored with golf. I would play in the dark and even in snow if I had to, just to get a few holes in. In fact I hallucinated, as so many other aspiring weekend warriors have, that I would play on the Champions Tour some day. Pretty funny! Anyway, Kimberly didn't share my enthusiasm. She did however have a gorgeous golf swing—to the untrained eye, that is. It was poetry in motion. It reminded me of the languid and relaxed stroke of Ernie Els, and was a sheer pleasure to watch, right up to the point of impact. That's where things got ugly! Oftentimes, after scooping a chunk of earth from the manicured fairways, her club, with a sizable piece of sod on the face of it, would then scoot the ball down the fairway a discouragingly short distance. Not only was she frustrated with her performance, she was causing herself a lot of physical pain from beating on the ground with her club. In short, she developed a really, really bad association with playing golf. But rather than abandon it and disregard it as something we would forever do apart, she signed us both up for a 3-day golf clinic at a top 100 golf academy. In 3 short days, she transformed her swing (now it is beautiful and effective) and turned golf into an activity that we will enjoy together as long as we can walk. In fact, she likes it more than I do now. Go figure!

Collaboration at a higher level is choosing to grow together and build your relationship toolbox. If you can agree to work together on improving your health, adding exercise to your daily routine, enhancing your sex life, growing your communication skills, increasing the passion in your life, or taking your earning capacity up a notch, you move together in a common direction with similar indoctrination. It becomes easier to relate and have fun together, and you always have something to talk about. But most importantly, you are both growing as individuals and as a couple. Consistently spending quality time together where you are both enjoying and sharing experiences is one of the most collaborative things I can think of. Collaboration is collectively "choosing" your marriage and refusing to settle for mediocrity. It's working together towards a common end.

"Collaboration at a higher level is choosing to grow together and build your relationship toolbox."

I think raising children is the most important activity to daily choose to collaborate together on. Nothing can challenge a relationship like children which makes it even more important to show a united front, act consistently with common values, and sort your differences out behind closed doors; not in front of the kids.

Riding a tandem bicycle is a powerful metaphor-in-action for collaboration in a relationship. You have 2 distinct positions on the bike, "Captain" and "Stoker." The Captain is determined by nature, not debate or flipping a coin.

The heaviest person goes in front (in the captain's seat) and is responsible for controlling the steering, braking, and avoiding obstacles. This is usually the man, but not always. The Stoker sits in the back and supports the efforts of the Captain in terms of navigation, pedal power, and "bogey" spotting.

"Collaboration is collectively "choosing" your marriage and refusing to settle for mediocrity." Tandem riders collaborate in that they are using the same mechanism to achieve similar goals. I say similar because as they both may want an exhilarating ride, their definitions of "an exhilarating ride" are usually quite different. He may want to push as hard as he can, while she might want to sightsee a bit. His effort to ride faster pulls her along with him. Her desire to sightsee and share what she sees gives "technicolor" to what otherwise might have been just a ride for him. The Stoker's confidence and belief in the Captain allows the Stoker to let go and enjoy the ride. The Captain's honor and respect for the Stoker allows her influence as to what is a comfortable speed and desirable route.

Tandem riding is a perfect metaphor of collaboration in marriage because it shows you how 2 distinctly different people can engage together in the same activity with very different, but symbiotically overlapping, agendas. Successful tandem riding is a perfect illustration of natural opposites unified as a complementary team. Much like dancing, there is a constant push and pull where the partners are never very far apart in the journey toward a similar or common goal.

Kimberly and I have been riding a tandem for, dare I say, 20+ years. In that time we have engaged countless couples in conversation about the dynamics of riding a tandem. We have heard comments and exclamations over and over, ranging from couples saying things like, "We could never do that!" to "I don't trust him enough" to "That would destroy our marriage" to women saying, "I would never ride on the back. I need to be in control".

Now, because I am not a psychologist and haven't done controlled studies on this subject, I can only speculate that a couple's ability to enjoy riding a tandem together is indicative of the quality of the individuals, and the quality of their marriage. Saying that attempting to ride a tandem together regularly might destroy their marriage would be akin to a couple saying that attempting to build a house together might destroy their marriage. We have all heard about the couples who have split over the building of a custom home. It is never the process of building a house (or riding a tandem for that matter) that destroys a marriage. The process only reveals the weaknesses and deficiencies in the individuals in the relationship. It reveals ego, selfishness, lack of trust, impatience, communication issues, or lack of respect. It reveals the "problems" that may have been ignored or swept under the rug for years. It reveals the ignored opportunities for personal growth.

I absolutely love riding our tandem and now with our daughter, our triplet. This experience commenced 22 years ago after our first bike ride together on single bikes. It was a beautiful sunny Saturday morning in Colorado with great expectations for a bike ride, Kimberly style. That is, sightseeing, pedaling and coasting downhill. My husband on the other hand, had planned to build muscle, gain endurance and physical strength. As he zoomed ahead of me, the idea of a "together" activity quickly vanished.

Shortly thereafter, we purchased our first tandem. Though I've learned to pedal when one should be coasting; he gets all the strength he desires riding and I enjoy my sightseeing, while engaged in what we consider a dynamic conversation that's mutually beneficial to both. I love filling 2 needs at once—exercise and quality time.

So, how *does* one grow? Let's explore this further in the next chapter.

ACTION STEPS

1. What are the things you would like to do together with your mate to learn how to collaborate better and grow your partnership?
2. Make a list of the things that get your partner interested and excited, and sign up for something they like.
3. As a couple, what would you like to see improved—your communication, health, sex life, finances, anything else? Find ways to improve your partnership in a collaborative way that challenges you, individually and as a couple.

THE ART OF GROWING UP

WE ENDED SECTION 2 with the cliffhanger idea that we can only have sex up to our level of personal development. That isn't completely true. More accurately, we can only have sex with someone who we are emotionally intimate with, up to our level of personal development.

In other words, it's often more likely for a person to have *mind-blowing* sex during a one-night stand than with the person they are in a "committed" relationship with. Don't throw the book down. I'm just stating a fact. This is really sad but often very true because, when we are with a stranger, we relinquish many of our hang-ups, and bypass our emotional traumas and barriers that prevent us from being completely open and authentic with our mates. We're able to do this because we want to have a good time, are caught up in the moment, aren't concerned with being judged or criticized, and have a need to express ourselves without fear of judgment or rejection.

Why are we often *not* able to have this experience with our mate? Because, as "under-matured" and poorly developed human beings, we cannot bear to reveal our authentic selves to our mate, nor can we unconditionally love and honor our mate when they reveal their authentic self.

This is why a couple's sex life is a window into the health and wellbeing of their relationship. One's level of personal development translates directly to their capacity to openly and authentically connect sexually with their partner. It also has a direct influence on whether their partner even desires them enough to have sex with them. As previously revealed, your growth and unfolding as a person plays a key role in maintaining the attraction, desire and magnetism your mate has for you over time. Over time, sex becomes less about resolving sexual tension (getting off) and more about the

"One's level of personal development translates directly to their capacity to openly and authentically connect sexually with their partner."

desire to share, experience and explore with your mate and lover—kind of like eating and drinking.

As your palate develops in sophistication, filling your stomach isn't just about satisfying hunger and meeting nutritional needs, it's more about deriving pleasure and enjoyment from the subtleties and nuances of new and unfamiliar flavors and preparations. The French have had this figured out for a long time. The connection between desire and growth in a marriage is so profound that you're going to wonder how anyone can experience a deep level of passion without the benefit of being in a long-term committed relationship.

So, how does one grow? Well, there is no one best or right way. In fact, there are infinite ways. It all comes down to how you respond to the circumstances, rubs and frictions in your marriage, and in your life.

We've covered so many different facets of relationship up to this point that if you simply embraced, honored and incorporated a few of them into your life, you would experience measurable improvement in your relationship. Even just recognizing that marriage "problems" are perfectly normal gives you a perspective that helps keep you engaged and thinking. Seeing them as welcome "challenges" takes you to an even higher level. Acknowledging that personal development comes from how you respond, adapt, grow and evolve in response to the challenges in your relationship is a monumental achievement for most people. The awareness you now have, gives you a whole new level of consciousness and accountability to yourself. But how does one actually grow?

I know I'm growing when the challenges of yesterday are not the same as today's. When you're faced with a challenge you must meet it head on. You don't avoid it or procrastinate addressing it, but brainstorm on what to do differently, take action and adjust as necessary until you achieve the results you desire.

The Marriage Paradox

By now you're grasping the paradoxical nature of marriage. Women and men, both—you can't live with 'em and you can't live without 'em. The very things that attract you together in the beginning, can later drive you apart. The "problems" you think you have, are actually blessings in disguise. The more emotionally fused you become, the more you fight, and the harder it is to maintain passion and eroticism.

"What?" you might be thinking.

Well, here is where we start to bring this all together. Remember that what makes a marriage good are things like love and emotional connection, because they give you certainty and security. But what makes a marriage passionate is a healthy level of uncertainty and variety. What keeps you magnetized to each other is the ever-present allure and mystery of your lover developing as a human being. Repeating a concept from the last section, desire and attraction is born in the "space" between 2 polar opposites. If we are to reconcile the paradox of having needs for both love and passion, certainty and variety, security and excitement; we need to resolve our confusion between love and merging as a couple.

The secret to doing this is a process called *differentiation*. The secret to maintaining healthy polarizing combinations of certainty and uncertainty, security and excitement, and love and passion in a long-term relationship is in differentiation.

"The 'problems' you think you have, are actually blessings in disguise." In his book *Passionate Marriage*, Dr. Schnarch suggests that when we couple up, we tend to naturally gravitate to someone with a similar level of differentiation. Simply put, we start out being a good match for each other. The challenges arise when we don't individually grow in our differentiation, or when one of us greatly outpaces the other in our differentiation. In other words, if just one of us matures intellectually, spiritually and sexually over time, it can become challenging to continue sharing together on a deeply intimate level. The reason for this is that differentiation implies a transcendence to higher and higher levels of consciousness. More on this in the next chapter.

Differentiation

Differentiation is the process of growing up, maintaining and growing yourself and your sense of self, while simultaneously connecting and bonding with others. It's the ability to be close to another human being yet maintain your separateness.

Differentiation is the process of developing the ability to unconditionally love another, accept another, respect another, and honor another without having to agree with them. It's the ability to honor and respect the beliefs, perspectives and preferences of another without feeling like you are dishonoring or compromising your own.

Paradoxically, differentiation is being able to get closer to your mate than ever before while simultaneously growing in your own sense of individuality and uniqueness. A highly differentiated person doesn't have to have her/his spouse agree with them to be happy. They are unshakeable and don't upset easily because their sense of self is independent of their mate. In other words, their identity isn't dependent on the relationship. In his book *Healing for Damaged Emotions*, David Seamands stated something to the effect that marriage is the union of 2 emotionally mature, independent adults who choose to be together. In other words, marriage (in the ideal sense) is the union of 2 highly differentiated people who choose to be together. Just the knowing that you are with each other by choice is highly polarizing.

"Differentiation is the process of growing up; maintaining and growing yourself and your sense of self, while simultaneously connecting and bonding with others."

The opposite of being differentiated is when someone has a highly *reflected sense of self*. This is when your mate's beliefs, ideas, behaviors, reactions and decisions become a reflection to you of who and what you are. Having a highly *reflected sense of self* can be extremely bonding (fusing), but with negative side effects. If your mate has an opinion that you disagree with, you think that somehow their opinion is a reflection of you, so it irks you. Or if they have a behavior that embarrasses you in public, your embarrassment stems from seeing them as a reflection of yourself.

The other side of *reflected sense of self* is in how it promotes sameness. A poorly differentiated person will unwittingly follow their parent's religion, become a lawyer because dad expects them to take over his law firm, or toss their dreams aside for the sake of their relationship.

Undifferentiated people tend to mirror each other's habits, adopt their preferences and abdicate to their mate's wants and desires in an effort to be loved, accepted and avoid conflict. Their identity is a direct reflection of the connection, or lack of connection, they have with their significant other.

A fun example of poor differentiation was in the movie *Runaway Bride* starring Julia Roberts and Richard Gere. The character Julia played was terrified of committing to a relationship when she knew her fiancée was in love with what was merely a figment of her true self. The fact was, she had never really discovered who she really was, so she just became whatever she thought would make her boyfriend love her. In this case, it was always adopting the tastes and preferences of her beau at the time. This was demonstrated by the fact that she always ordered her eggs in whatever preparation her current boyfriend happened to prefer them. When individuals do this in a committed relationship, they stymie their personal growth, become un-interesting, and depolarize themselves to their mate.

Differentiation doesn't mean always doing your own thing without thought of your mate's needs—to the contrary. A highly differentiated person meets their mate's needs at a high level. They are just able to do it without sacrificing their sense of self, or feeling like they have sold themselves out. A highly differentiated person may forego meeting his own needs or even operating by his own rules, but they do it by choice and out of the desire to support the other rather than from a place of deference or abdication.

This ability to harmoniously and even ecstatically coexist with a uniquely different human being happens when, as Robert Kegan explains in his book *In Over Our Heads*, we ascend to a level of consciousness where we realize that who we *think* we are is merely a construct of our own imaginations. Once it dawns on us that the values, beliefs and standards that we each have and that we think make up who we are, are merely superficial preferences to be changed, altered and evolved like one might change their outfit or wardrobe, the trivial and mundane "issues" that would normally upset us or cause us frustration simply evaporate. This happens when we move from being offended and frustrated by our differences to honoring and appreciating our differences.

"A highly differentiated person meets their mate's needs at a high level."

Integration

Integration is the other side of the *differentiation* coin. If differentiation is the process of discovering, growing and maintaining your separate "self", *integration* is the process of intimately connecting that "self" with others in a meaningful way. A way to sum up *integration* is in the statement, "What's important to you is important to me because it's important to you." This means that you want for your mate what your mate wants, instead of you wanting for your mate what *you* want for them. Another way of saying this is that because you love someone, you want to support them and be a part of what's important to them, *because* it's important to them. An example of this might be a willingness to attend Catholic Church services with your mate even though you were raised a Protestant. This is an example of how you can show support without agreeing. You don't have to agree to feel the love and connection that comes from being the giver, or the recipient, of the gift.

An example of integration from my own relationship is the fact that my wife loves to dance and I don't. I grew up in a non-dancing family. More accurately, I grew up in an anti-dancing family. I was taught that dancing is an abominable act. I don't view it that way anymore but nevertheless, I don't have any natural desire to get out on a dance floor and wiggle my body. When the music starts playing, my hips don't start rocking and my foot doesn't start tapping. It just hasn't done anything for me (historically). In fact, there was a time that I could think of 100 things (including hard labor) I would rather do than dance. For Kimberly, on the other hand, dancing is as natural as walking. It lights her up like a Christmas tree. When she's out on the dance floor, I can tell she's connecting with and releasing her authentic self. She is in her femininity.

So what is integration? It's spending time with your mate doing activities that light them up even if you don't naturally enjoy them. It's supporting your mate in those things that are important to them even if they aren't important to you. It's making what's important to your mate, important to you. And when you do this consistently, your expansion and growth go into turbo mode.

So, what's the most loving and integrating thing I can do for Kimberly when it comes to dancing? Sign us up for some Salsa or Swing dance lessons! When I do this, the effect is explosive. I grow and stretch myself like crazy because I'm doing something I would never otherwise do; I expand my capacity to love Kimberly without condition; Kimberly lights up like a Christmas tree because she's doing something that resonates with her at a deep level; Kimberly's desire for me magnifies because I've done something for her that she knows is hard for me; and finally, I develop a new appreciation for something that was previously off my radar. Who knows, I may even develop a love for something I previously shied from, and I did this out of my desire to truly *love* my wife.

Putting it all together

Remember when I suggested that in most marriages, a couple's sex life is made up of leftovers? I then said that the object is to expand your sexual repertoire so that eventually there is nothing left over you won't do. Well, this requires both differentiation and integration.

It requires differentiation from the standpoint that you have to grow to break through personal barriers and rules that might limit you sexually. And it requires integration in that you are always willing to support your mate in meeting their needs, even if they don't resonate with you. In other words, you are willing to at least dip your toe in the water of your mate's desire pool because you have chosen to love and support them. And in doing so, you support your own expansion and personal growth. This isn't just about sex. In fact it's mostly not about sex. A well differentiated and integrated couple collaborates on a meaningful life together while supporting and involving themselves in the individual loves and pursuits of the other. I love the metaphor of each of you being supporting actors in the other's play of life. Some scenes will star your mate with you in a supporting role, and vice versa. But the best are the ones where you collaborate together as co-stars.

"A well differentiated and integrated couple collaborates on a meaningful life together while supporting and involving themselves in the individual loves and pursuits of the other."

A passionate marriage happens when you love what you know and see in your mate, and yet are allured and intrigued by what you don't see. This is what differentiation does for you and your marriage. It provides a dynamic much like a moon orbiting around a planet. The balance between the gravitational pull of the planet and the centrifugal force of the moon's orbit maintains a perfect "space" between the two. To maintain the relationship, the "pull" of the planet must be maintained as well as the movement of the moon. Differentiation is the process of simultaneously growing the space while decreasing it at the same time. It's discovering, growing and honoring the "you" in you, and in your mate. As Einstein said, "Life is like riding a bicycle. To keep your balance, you must keep moving." Differentiation is all about stretching, expansion and movement. And to have this experience requires personal growth.

"A passionate marriage happens when you love what you know and see in your mate, and yet are allured and intrigued by what you don't see."

Personal growth isn't easy or everyone would be doing it. It's difficult because it challenges your beliefs about who you are and your beliefs about what is possible. It forces you to confront your own self-imposed limitations and break through them. Basically, it calls you on all your bullshit. Marriage is the perfect environment for this. If you want to be the best that you can be and rise to the level of your highest potential, and you are married, you are in the right place. Because without the commitment that comes with marriage, you usually don't have enough leverage on your self to do what it takes to grow. That's why when you see those 60-year-old bachelors out there who have never been married, they often seem to have the emotional maturity of a 12-year-old. They just never had a reason to grow up.

So, how do we use our marriage as a tool for personal growth? The first step is to recognize that the conflicts and upsets that you have with your mate aren't really about your mate or even your marriage, they're usually about you. When we learn to honor and respect our mate for what and who they are, and stop trying to change and manipulate them, we will be loving them at a higher level than ever before. When we realize that the tensions and rubs that we have with them stem from our own lack of differentiation, we will see everything in a new light.

A Great Marriage Is a Choice

Once you acknowledge and choose to use every problem or difficulty as an opportunity to do a self-assessment instead of reacting, complaining, manipulating or stonewalling your mate, your expansion is inevitable.

Remember the story of the Procrustean bed where Procrustes either stretched or cut off the limbs of his guests in order to fit them to his guest beds perfectly? Well, that is exactly what we are doing to our mate when we respond to them with any behavior other than unconditional love. We are trying to change them and manipulate them through our anger, impatience or withdrawal, all of which are forms of marital sadism. This kind of behavior is what stymies personal growth and leads to what are often referred to as "irreconcilable differences."

What are "irreconcilable differences"? According to the courts it means that no one party is responsible for the divorce. Nonsense! Marriage doesn't fail, the 2 people in the marriage fail to grow and expand. If you don't agree with your mate about certain things agree to disagree; then get creative on how to move forward together in harmony, respectfully honoring each other's points of view.

Once you've adopted this new awareness and acknowledged that problems are your opportunity to evolve, the next step is to exercise your power of choice. You choose your love for your mate over your need to be right. You choose your marriage over your friends. You choose your relationship over your pride. You choose your love over your difference of opinion. You choose to respond differently than you have before. You choose to act from your highest and best self. You choose laughter over anger. You choose patience over temper. You choose silence over yelling. You choose to focus on what is really important and defocus on the petty, meaningless minutia that so often rub us raw. You choose to be the person your mate deserves. You choose to love even when you don't feel loved. You choose to treat your mate like a prize worthy of your pursuit.

Learning to make these choices doesn't come easy at first. It's kind of like building muscle. It takes consistent dedication and a lot of repetition. Sometimes you just don't feel like doing it but you do it anyway. Because if you don't, you know you are settling for a low standard and that's not who you are.

The first workout is always the hardest to do, but after a while you begin to thrive on it because you can feel the difference and see the difference. You develop self-confidence and self-assuredness. You are more capable, more flexible and more resilient. You are becoming unshakeable.

"When we realize that the tensions and rubs that we have [with our mates] stem from our own lack of differentiation, we will see everything in a new light."

As you are defining and honing (differentiating) yourself, your mate sees and feels the difference, and it piques their interest. They are relieved, curious and magnetized for 2 reasons. First, you are shedding the skin of destructive behaviors that caused them pain and frustration on some level; and second, you are revealing an evolved version of yourself that they haven't seen before. They are feeling a new level of certainty from the love that you've demonstrated by your new behavior, while simultaneously feeling a polarizing level of uncertainty that comes with the unveiling of your higher self. Do you see the magic in this? What would your marriage look like if this dynamic were to go on as long as you both shall live? What if you were to engage in this process together collaboratively?

To a poorly differentiated person, this dynamic might seem scary or intimidating instead of exciting and exhilarating. Poorly differentiated people don't like change, especially in their mate. A poorly differentiated person finds certainty in stagnation, sameness and predictability. That's why they will often stay in an unfulfilling, or even toxic, relationship even if it means enduring emotional or physical pain. At least they have the certainty of having someone in their life. Individuals with a highly reflected sense of self don't support the evolution of their mate because their reflection keeps changing and they find this unsettling.

Feeling caution, trepidation or resistance to a mate's growth and unfolding as a human being is a signal for one's own need for growth, maturity and self-realization. If this is you, it's time to jump out of the airplane. At first you may feel terrified, and then, if only for a moment, you'll drop into a zone of excitement, awe, wonder, contentment and peace. Stay with it and you'll get a glimpse of the bliss that is yours; yours when you love completely, live true to your feminine or masculine essence, and stay on the path of growing into your highest and best self.

Wow! Up to this point, we've laid the foundation for attraction, desire and passion in a committed relationship. If you haven't figured it out on your own, your attraction and desire for each other happens primarily in your mind, not from a response to a visual or physical stimuli. It happens because we love and are loved; we want and feel wanted; we pursue and are pursued; we love what we know about the other and are intrigued by what we don't; we are witnessing the unveiling of an evolving human being and are awed by it; and we feel honor, respect, gratitude and appreciation for our mate because we know that they chose us and continue to do so each day.

We've learned that by consciously choosing them on a daily basis, our attention and intention becomes biased to supporting the needs of our mate and lover. This is the foundation for a deeply passionate and spiritually sexual connection. It's not about trading security for sex or relieving a primal urge anymore. You don't even need a hormonal desire for it—as you get older, you may not even *have* a hormonal desire for it. You're with this person because you crave them and want to connect with their mind, heart and soul. Collaborating on life with them provides you with all the "juice" you could ever want in a relationship. It's not so much about sex as it is about really wanting the one you are with. And when you make love in this state, it transcends the physical to the spiritual realm.

This seems like a good place to stop but we're going to take this one level higher. We want to seal the deal, complete the paradigm shift, demolish the Procrustean marital bed, and trade it for a honeymoon suite with a revolving bed and heart-shaped hot tub. We want you to fall in love over and over again. But first, we want to share with you a *Secret*.

ACTION STEPS

1. Remember that marriage "problems" are actually just opportunities for you to grow yourself. Start reframing your "problems" as challenges and start looking for ways that you can take your own personal development up a notch.

2. Identify some of the differences between you and your spouse that are really just gender differences or merely preferences. Think about how silly it is to argue, bicker and get frustrated over the very things that make you each unique and polarizing. Then view them with a new sense of honor, respect and even humor.

3. Meditate on the idea that "growing up" is the constant and never-ending process of developing your own authentic self while

simultaneously honoring and supporting your mate's own authentic evolution, even if it doesn't perfectly parallel yours.

4. Come up with 3 things that are really important to your mate that you haven't been supportive of. Choose the one that you know would absolutely light them up the most, then take a huge step forward to make that happen for them. This is what you signed up for. This is what keeping your vows is all about. Meeting your mate's needs (keeping your vows) is all about growing your self.

5. Remember that how you respond to anything your mate does is a choice. Choose your relationship over your pride. Choose your love over your difference of opinion. Choose to respond differently than you have before. Choose to act from your highest and best self. Choose laughter over anger. Choose patience over temper. Choose to focus on what is really important and defocus on the petty, meaningless minutia that so often rubs us raw. Choose to be the person your mate deserves. You choose to love even when you don't feel loved. You choose to treat your mate like a prize worthy of your pursuit.

THE SECRET

WHAT DO THE BOOKS *Think and Grow Rich* by Napoleon Hill, *The Secret* by Rhonda Byrne, *The Power of Intention* by Wayne Dyer and *The Holy Bible* have in common? They all share a philosophy, an insight, a message, a secret; a secret so powerful that it has been hidden in plain sight so that only those with "eyes to see and ears to hear" have been entrusted with its power; a secret so profound that it has been veiled from the masses in story, poetry, parable and metaphor. Every great leader, teacher, philosopher, seer, alchemist and innovator past and present, knows it. It's the force behind all meaningful innovation, progress and evolution. It's the secret to realizing whatever you want in your life. It holds the key to manifesting such things as health, wealth, wellbeing, and yes, having a beautiful, exciting, rewarding and even passionate marriage.

The secret is to desire something so strongly that you get crystal clear on what you want; you then align your focus, your thoughts, and your actions for the support and accomplishment of your desire. In other words, you first develop a clear vision of what you want, and then you start managing your focus, making choices, modifying behaviors and taking actions that are in alignment with that vision.

If you aren't crystal clear on what you want, you're guaranteed to get something you don't want. The bible says that without a vision, the people will perish. Without a vision for your marriage, your marriage will perish. That isn't to say that it isn't possible to have a good marriage without a vision. Many couples have good marriages by default. They just happen to have the right temperaments, personalities, moral fortitude and love to make it work. But who wants their marriage to just "work"? If you want an exciting, deeply meaningful and passionate marriage, you need to be married with mindfulness, with purpose and with intention. You need to decide what you want, what you need to do to get it and most importantly, who you need to become to attract it.

In the case of *your* marriage, what is *your* desire? What do you want your marriage to look like? In order to be crystal clear about this, you need to get specific and even graphic about what this means to you. If your vision is foggy and uninspiring, you not only won't be able to determine how to achieve it, you won't be motivated to achieve it. It's not enough to say that you want a "good marriage" or even a "passionate marriage". You've got to paint the picture in living color, describing vivid details that compel you, inspire you and motivate you. Don't feel bad if this feels strange or difficult. It's often hard for people to get going with this so let me give you some help.

Oftentimes, it's easier for people to conceptualize what they want by first identifying what they don't want. They're more in touch with what causes them pain than what gives them pleasure. If this is you, make a list of what it is that causes you the most pain and frustration in your relationship, and then think of what the polar opposite of that is and what that would look like. To do this, you may have to disassociate yourself from your present situation or you'll find yourself setting your sights way too low. If a woman is dying of starvation and thirst, she's going to be wishing for bread and water, not Gorgonzola-crusted filet mignon with organic fire-roasted Yukon Gold garlic, mashed potatoes accompanied by a Chateau Lafite Rothschild 1984 Bordeaux. It's hard to think about what you really want if you could have anything, when your most basic needs aren't being met.

Here's a hypothetical, but rather typical, example of this to help you understand what I mean. A big source of frustration for some might be that after 15 years with the same person, they are virtually in a sexless marriage. If they haven't had sex with their mate for 3 months or 3 years; or maybe when they do have sex on that rare occasion, it leaves them feeling frustrated and disappointed; or their disappointing sex life has left them with a negative association with sex with their mate. If any one of these scenarios is the case, it can be difficult to envision having mind-blowing sex that leaves them feeling like they met God. Just having sex, any kind of sex, on a regular basis might seem like a worthy aspiration.

So, if you make a list of what you want to eliminate in your relationship, stretch your imagination and paint a detailed picture of what the opposite of that is. If you can preferably go straight to painting your grand vision for your marriage without having to go to the painful side, more power to you. Just don't feel bad if you can't. And keep in mind that there is no perfect. Perfection is a poor standard because it's unattainable. That said, I tell my wife all the time that she's perfect for me; and what I mean is that in that moment, I feel like she is the only one for me because I am crazy attracted to her, feel blessed by her infinite love and patience, or I feel like she is driving me out of my mind, i.e., playing a collaborative role in my own evolution as a human being.

Here are some questions to help you start creating your vision. Use them to help you identify the part your marriage will play in bringing joy, meaning, certainty, excitement, fulfillment, adventure and passion into your life. Think about the part your marriage can play in meeting your physical, emotional and spiritual needs. Remember, think big and think in vivid detail.

1. In my dream marriage, what does my daily communication with my mate look like? What is our communication and connection like when we are engaged in family activities? What is our communication and connection like when we are in a social environment? What is our communication and connection like when we are in our separate work environs?

2. How often and how much time will we spend together daily, weekly and monthly having focused one-on-one quality time together?

3. What does our sex life look like? How often do we have it? Where do we have it? What is the experience like? What does the evolution of our sex life look like? How do we feel before, during and after? What are the lingering effects?

4. Who am I as a human being in all of this, and how can I describe the role I play in attracting this into my life? In other words, what quality of person are we in our roles as husband/wife, lover, collaborator, confidant, partner, mate, priest/priestess, guardian, etc.

5. What is the grand purpose of our marriage that may go beyond just meeting our own needs? How might we use it to influence future generations or make the world a better place? How can we use it as a platform for change?

6. How do I want to express my inner romantic, my inner priest/priestess, my inner comedian, my inner leader, etc.?

Here's a page from my own journal as an example.

I want my marriage to be my life's ultimate experience. Knowing the role it plays in my development as a person and in my ability to meet my 7 core needs, I want to juice it for all it's worth. I want to be in love with, and polarized by, my woman and her with me. I want to be a little on the edge of my seat, not always knowing quite what to expect as I spend my life watching her blossom as a human being. I see us collaborating and synergizing together as we support each other in the pursuit of our collective and individual paths. I want to live each day in the consciousness that we have chosen each other, keeping the other in our thoughts, intentions and prayers.

I consciously make an effort to help my husband have an awesome daily experience. I think about little things that I can incorporate into our schedule that will put a smile on his face, make his life easier and, on occasion, add some surprise and intrigue.

We'll communicate frequently with touch, whisper and eye contact when in close proximity, and by phone/text when apart; always letting the other know they are our #1. I see us honoring and embracing our differences in perspective in a way that turns them into a source of comedy, adventure and insight, instead a source of pain and frustration. When we disagree, we'll never lose sight of what's really important; never allowing the trivia and mundane to be a focus. We'll always stay in close communication so that the other never has any uncertainty or confusion about what is going on in our lives. If and when we do feel uncertainty, it's because we don't know what exciting event or surprise the other is planning to bring into our day whether it be in the kitchen, in the bedroom or in the form of personal development, personal adornment, romance, sexual novelty or spiritual insight.

I make a weekly and monthly plan that touches on each one of these things. If you schedule it, it will become real; if you just think about it, it's only a dream.

I want my life with her to be inspiring, compelling, challenging and adventurous. I want it to play out like a cinema movie combining comedy, drama, adventure, action, eroticism and spiritual epiphany. Think Six Days Seven Nights meets The Da Vinci Code meets Under the Tuscan Sun meets The Celestine Prophecy meets Fifty Shades of Grey. To manifest this, I need to consistently be growing into the highest and best version of myself that I can conjure up. This means developing the husband/romantic/lover/father/friend/leader/wizard/priest/comedian facets of my personality that play key roles in the production of my life.

I love the premeditation of so many of our incredible experiences together, but also love our flexibility to "just go with it" and let surprise, adventure and uncertainty add its spice.

As a husband, I want to be the man my wife deserves. In fact, I want Rock Star status. I want to be the man she wants, desires and is proud to have chosen as her man. I not only want to provide for her physical and financial needs, I want to fill her emotionally and spiritually.

As a romantic, I want to pursue my wife like she's the catch of a lifetime. I want her to think, "God, the way he's pursuing me, I must be one hot catch!" I want to enjoy the cat &

mouse pursuit of each other that most couples enjoy only in the beginning. I want to be enticed, compelled and tantalized into the present… into the moment. I want to treat my wife like one treats a lover, and experience the expectation and variety that comes with being in an exciting love affair. On a daily basis, I'll make it a point to make sure she knows I'm after her and desiring her. On no less than a weekly basis, we'll enjoy romantic mornings, afternoons or evenings that include uninterrupted, mutually enjoyable activities. At least 3 times a year, I want to enjoy weekend getaways where we can newly reconnect without any of the distractions of being home, and renew our commitment and fervor to each other.

As a lover, I want to love and be loved from the heart and soul, and not the head. I want to learn to give and receive completely, without limit or boundary, and with total presence. I want to grow our hearts, minds and skills as a couple so that we might experience glimpses of the divine through our sexual union. I want to take my lady places she has never been before so that she wonders every time we have sex, "Why don't we do this every day?"

It amazes me, how common it is for couples to put life ahead of sex. However, when you engage with your mate at a transcendental level, it's addictive and you will wonder why you let the opportunity for even one encounter to slip away.

As a father, I want to be the World's Greatest Dad. And not because I show our daughter a good time or give her what she wants, but because I give her what she needs most from me, my unconditional love and my time. I want to share a deep love with her that carries us through the challenges of her growing up. I want to learn the lessons that she has for me so that I might be the dad she deserves and grow to become the person that only a child can help me become. I want to learn to love her unconditionally in a way that fosters deep connection that lasts her lifetime. I want her to feel comfortable telling me anything, knowing that I will respond with love, patience and kindness. I hope that her observation of my own choices and behaviors will set a standard for her of moral fortitude and ethics. Finally, I have to say that I want to be a great dad because I know it turns my wife on.

As a friend I want to be Kimberly's best, she certainly is mine.

As a leader, I want to have the strength, courage and wisdom to guide my family through the minefields of life. If I am called upon to build a shopping mall using a Q-tip and a pocketknife, I'll be up for the challenge. As a leader, I want to be able to use good judgment in all things, weighing in all available information, perspectives, and individual needs when making decisions or recommendations. As a leader, I want to be sympathetic and sensitive to the individual needs and desires of each family member. I want to remember that the wisdom I need to lead may come from anywhere, including our daughter.

As a wizard, I want to tap into my inner Merlin and create an environment of possibility and wonder for my family. I want to encourage and support their creativity and imagination, and support the knowing that anything is possible when you believe.

As a priest, I want to be a demonstration of unselfishness and selflessness, learning to live more in spirit and less in ego. I want to lead my family in prayers and meditations that cultivate thoughtful, conscious and intentional living.

As a comedian, I want to put a smile on everyone's face, and never a frown when it can be prevented. I want to learn to see the comedy in our relationship challenges and learn to laugh at things instead of getting frustrated. Comedians just see the world through a different lens than most people. I want to metaphorically carry around a pair of "comedian" glasses that I can put on in a pinch. I'll keep them right next to the rose-colored glasses I keep ready at all times.

I want to suggest creating this vision for your marriage individually, and then co-creating one collaboratively. Use it as a foundation to co-construct a marriage that is inspiring, fulfilling and compelling for you both. Curiously, most couples never actually sit down and go through this process. It seems like an obvious pre-marital step that we would take somewhere between falling in love and taking your vows. Having a shared vision for your marriage and your life will guide you like your GPS guides you to your destination on your smartphone. It doesn't mean that you can't collectively change your destination on the fly. That's the cool thing about setting goals and standards for your life. It gives you a target to daily set your sights on, and a frame of reference to guide your choices and decisions. But, the destination and the route you're going to take to get there may change over time as you evolve, grow and expand your frame of reference. When we take a family road trip for example, we almost never get to where we planned on going because we find ourselves enjoying the journey and the diversions along the way.

The incomparable Zig Ziglar once said that the quality of a marriage is a reflection of the quality of the people in the marriage. He believed strongly that the wrong person could be turned into the right person, or even the right person turned into the wrong person, simply by the quality (or lack thereof) of love, energy and intention that we bring to the relationship. That's why in my own vision, I put so much emphasis on becoming the kind of person who magnetizes, attracts and manifests the kind of marriage I want and the kind of life I want. Kimberly and I collaborate to create compelling visions for our marriage, our family and our business life. We then individually and collaboratively work to become the individuals and the team that synergistically lives within the context of the common vision.

Remember the tandem metaphor we discussed earlier? I summed it up by saying, "Tandem riding is a perfect metaphor of collaboration in marriage because it shows you how 2 distinctly different people can engage together in the same activity with very different, but symbiotically overlapping, agendas. Successful tandem riding is a perfect illustration of natural opposites unified as a complementary team. Much like dancing, there is a constant push and pull where the partners are never very far apart in the journey toward a similar or common goal." Not only are you meeting each other's needs, you're meeting them at an exponentially higher level than you ever could on your own and you're growing like crazy in the process. That's what marriage is all about. That's what life is all about.

To reiterate the premise of this chapter, "The secret is to desire something so strongly that you get crystal clear on what you want; you then align your focus, your thoughts, and your actions for the support and accomplishment of your desire. In other words, you first develop a clear vision of what you want, and then you start managing your focus, making choices, modifying behaviors and taking actions that are consistent with that vision."

You can download a *Marriage Vision Template* under RESOURCES>FORMS at www.GreatMarriageGreatLife.com

Behind your vision you need a powerful and compelling *WHY*; a driving force that daily inspires you to do whatever it takes to realize what you want at its highest level. Creating a compelling vision for your marriage is the first step in harnessing the power of this *desire*. The next step is to develop reasons why realizing your vision is a *must* and not an option for you.

In the chapter entitled "Why you know what to do, but don't do it!," we discussed the importance of having a compelling reason behind getting what you want, and how identifying a greater purpose will give you the leverage you need on yourself to push beyond your self-imposed limitations. Examples of the *WHY* for me are:

1. Because my wife deserves a man who loves and accepts her unconditionally

2. Because my wife deserves to feel adored and cherished
3. Because my wife is a goddess and she deserves a counterpart who inspires and challenges her
4. Because I want my wife to love her life with me
5. Because being less than my best causes my lover pain and suffering
6. Because I value my integrity and I feel totally incongruent when I'm not fulfilling my vows to my wife
7. Because I want to practice what I preach and be congruent as a marriage coach and educator
8. Because my wife entrusted herself to me to walk with her in partnership toward her own spiritual awakening
9. Because I want to have the energy to fill my woman's needs at a high level
10. Because I want to live a long, healthy and vibrant life together and not cause unnecessary hardship on my wife because I didn't take care of myself
11. Because I want to be the one who brings joy, laughter, excitement and adventure to her life and not some other man
12. Because I want the feeling of being in love
13. Because I want to live a life of passion, fulfillment and meaning with a woman by my side who inspires me, excites me, awes me, and humbles me
14. Because I want to be a force for good by inspiring a global paradigm shift for how people view marriage and the nature of the relationship between men and women
15. Because I want to live/be/experience life from a place of love, beauty, grace, wonder, mystery and awe where the petty and mundane cease to be a part of my awareness.

Now, develop your own compelling WHY. Once you have your Vision and your Why, the next step is to align your thoughts, decisions and actions with your vision. Every great philosopher and human development personality including, but not limited to, Plato, Ben Franklin, Thomas Jefferson, Abraham Lincoln, Napoleon Hill, Nelson Mandela, Zig Ziglar, Tony Robbins and Deepak Chopra reveal the secret to manifesting what you want in your life.

When you put your intention and attention into something; act and behave as if it is real; the universe conspires to make it a reality.

Within the pages of this book are the tools, insights and distinctions you need to realize the passionate, fulfilling and purposeful marriage you desire. And because you're not willing to settle for normal, and for less than your potential, you're ready to break free of the cultural, religious and societal conditioning laid down by your friends, family and predecessors, and venture into a realm of love, passion, sex and spiritual awareness that comes only with growing upwards toward the highest version of ourselves.

"[Your marriage is] a vehicle for transcendence to a higher level of thinking, a deeper experience, and a profound way of contributing to the future of humanity."

Your marriage is more than just a fractional component of your life as in you grow up, go to college, pursue a career, couple up, have kids, retire and die. It's a vehicle for transcendence to a higher level of thinking, a deeper experience, and a profound way of contributing to the future of humanity. Now that's a vision worth having!

ACTION STEPS

1. Using the list of questions in this chapter to kick-start you, create a vision of what you would like to manifest in your various roles in life.
2. What are your supporting 'whys' for creating and upholding your vision in these practical, emotional and spiritual aspects of your life? These 'whys' will become the driving force behind everything you want to accomplish in your relationship.

FLOW AND THE ART OF FALLING IN LOVE

Falling in love is easy. Falling in love with the same person repeatedly is extraordinary.

—Crystal Woods

Yes, couples can fall in love over and over again. And yes, it is *extra-ordinary*. Extraordinary is defined as: going beyond what is ordinary, usual, regular, normal, or customary and exceptional to a very marked extent. Synonyms include words like uncommon, incredible, sensational, stunning, astounding, amazing and phenomenal. Falling in love with the same person repeatedly *is* extraordinary, rare, deeply fulfilling, and very attainable. It might be the richest experience you can have. Your capacity to evolve yourself and contribute to your family, community and the world at large grows exponentially as a result.

So how do we not only stay in love, but actually fall in love over and over again? Is it even possible? American journalist Mignon McLaughlin once said that, "A successful marriage requires falling in love many times, [but] always with the same person." I wholeheartedly agree with Ms. McLaughlin and would like to expand on her statement with a little re-write.

*A passionate marriage is falling in love over and over with the same person, **albeit a new version of that person**.*

—Tad Horning

If you searched the internet for the ingredients to staying in love, you'll find lists that include things like: be kind to each other, give each other attention, spend quality time together, be a good listener and act like you did when you were dating. These are all great skills and qualities that *in-love* couples have and we've touched on them all thus far in this book. They are all things that couples do when they love each other whether they do it with intention or by default. They are all hallmarks of a "good" marriage.

That said, as we've all internalized by now, "good" is often not good enough for some people at some point in time in their growth and development. That's because a "good" marriage isn't necessarily passionate, exciting, inspiring or compelling. Like the woman mentioned at the beginning of Chapter 4, sometimes, having love *just isn't* enough. As evolving human beings, we need to be stimulated, challenged and inspired. We often want to experience the juice of *falling* in love. We crave the chemical high that accompanies newness, excitement, adventure, mystery and uncertainty. We want to tingle. We want to be magnetized. We want to want, and to be wanted. We want to feel alive! We want to be *in love*.

Falling in love has been likened to temporary insanity. Insanity is the state of being out of one's mind. Temporary implies that it is a transitory or fleeting state. Falling in love has

> *"Being in love might be likened to being slightly out of one's mind indefinitely rather than temporarily."*

always implied some level of ecstatic euphoria, whereas being in love has carried connotations of a milder, yet enduring, experience. *Being in love* might be likened to being slightly out of one's mind indefinitely rather than temporarily.

The experience of being in love and the desire for the feelings associated with falling in love, set us up for getting married and sometimes tempt us to get unmarried in a quest to re-experience the tension that comes with the excitement and mystery of being with a new person. At some point, we get tired of just living and want to feel alive again. We tire of just loving and want to experience the novelty and euphoria of falling in love.

This leads us to the billion-dollar question that culminates the content of this book. *How do we fall in love over and over again with the same person?*

The answer to this profound question is what our online training and live events are all about. In this book, I have been attempting to answer what we usually convey in person with a compelling energy, passion and dynamic that has real efficacy. The reason I say this is that reading a book is kind of like reading the lyrics of a song. As meaningful as they may be, they don't convey the power and emotion you experience when you actually hear the song sung by a human voice, even if it is through the medium of an electronic device. However, there is nothing quite as transformational as going to a live concert.

The energy in a room of people connected by a collective love, intention and consciousness magnifies your experience, makes an indelible impression on your mind, and changes you in ways you don't expect. In short, live events can be transformational—even transcendent. We love holding them and we love going to them. That all said, let's give this a shot.

The *Falling in Love* potion has 2 parts. The first part is really about secular development and the second part is about spiritual development. Where one ends and the other begins is often fuzzy because, oftentimes, in order to grow our skills as a human being, we need to first grow ourselves as a spiritual being. So as we explore these, you'll initially see the distinction between the 2 but then it will start to feel as if they are inseparable. The first is about expanding your *self*, your personhood, your value and flavor as a human being; the second is about transcending the invention of your *self* and growing (letting go) in the actualization of your own divinity.

Be willing to let go of the current you; your beliefs, ideals, values, preferences and operating system that aren't really you, and be open to new beliefs, ideals, values and preferences that could be the next evolution of you.

When you combine this elevated level of consciousness with the constant and never-ending expansion of self, your experience will be nothing short of transcendent.

Part 1 - Personal Growth and the Expansion of Self

I want to restate the quote from page 180. *"A passionate marriage is falling in love over and over with the same person, albeit a new version of that person."* Note the emphasis on *a new version of that person*. Herein lies the secret to not only a passionate marriage, but also an extraordinary life.

In Part 1 of the formula for falling in love, we're going to focus on 2 really significant things; the first is the ability of our mind and body to produce and modulate the "feel good" chemicals in the body that are responsible for the feelings we associate with being in love, namely ecstasy, euphoria and bliss; and second, we're going to take a hard look at what is meant by, "...a new version of that person".

Wayne Dyer used to tell a funny story about having lunch with his good buddy, Deepak Chopra. If only I could have been a fly on the wall I might have witnessed a profound yet entertaining exchange about spirituality, the mind-body connection, and the body's ability to heal itself. On this particular occasion, Wayne tells of a waitress asking Deepak if he would like a cocktail, to which Deepak responded, "No thanks, I am making my own." What he was alluding to was the innate ability that he knew he had to regulate and release chemicals from his body's own built-in pharmacy. In effect, he was saying that he was mixing his own cocktail within his body.

The significance of this is astounding. Early on in our courtship as a couple, the initial attraction phase is followed by the phenomenon of falling in love. This "falling in love" stage is precipitated by our body's release of a magical chemical cocktail that includes the chemicals dopamine, oxytocin, endorphins, norepinephrine and anandamide. This elixir is responsible for the ecstasy, euphoria and bliss of falling in love.

Amongst other functions, *dopamine* is an organic chemical your body produces in response to pleasure. It makes you feel good, fully engages you in the moment, and essentially predisposes you to wanting more of whatever stimulus or activity prompted its release.

Oxytocin is a hormone known as the bonding chemical. It induces feelings of love and attachment.

Endorphins are brain chemicals known as neurotransmitters. They have the ability to reduce your perception of pain by interacting with your nervous system's opiate receptors similarly to how morphine or heroin would. Not only do endorphins reduce pain but they also have the added bonus of producing feelings of euphoria, and even boosting your immunity.

Norepinephrine is a neurotransmitter that brings you into the here and now. In other words, it gets you focused on the present. It readies your mind and body to put all your available resources into whatever activity you are engaged in that minute (or second) of your life.

Anandamide, sometimes referred to as the "bliss molecule", produces a "happy, bliss, joy" experience similar to that induced by the THC, the main psychoactive compound found in marijuana. Not only does it give you a heightened state of glee, it has antidepressant and anti-anxiety properties to boot.

Not only does this chemical cocktail induce you to become enamored with your lover, it serves to diminish your perception of their faults and imperfections. When under its powerful influence, you see your potential mate with rose-colored glasses. These special glasses are compliments of chemicals your body produces when you are courting for the sole purpose of, as some believe, the preservation of the human race. The dirty little trick is that your body naturally stops producing this love potion after 18-24 months, which up until the last 50 years, was more than enough time for any couple to fall in love, tie the knot, and get pregnant with their first child.

An enduring and passionate marriage is about making the quantum leap from the initial and involuntary, chemically-induced state of falling in love experienced at the beginning of a relationship, to the intentionally-induced experience of falling in love. The first is out of your control and completely autonomic (automatic, unconscious), the second is by design and alchemically crafted. The first is our initiation into the school of marriage mastery, of which most drop out; the second, our master's thesis.

In his ground-breaking book *Flow*, Mihaly Csikszentmihalyi explains how after studying diverse peoples all over the globe, he discovered that the happiest people on earth are the ones who feel like their lives have the most meaning. This sense of meaning came from consistently experiencing a state that he eventually called Flow. Some today refer to the Flow state as being "in the zone".

Those who experience Flow at a very high level, are those who have the most peak experiences, whether sometimes by accident or, more often, by design. Interestingly, the happiest people didn't just have the most peak experiences, they were found to work hard for those experiences, often devoting their lives to having these experiences. These experiences sometimes involved difficult, risky and even painful activities that pushed them to the limits of their minds and bodies. In other words, they were pushing themselves beyond their comfort zones, and tinkering with their own human potential. Interestingly enough, whether the Flow generating activities were inherently enjoyable, physically taxing or even dangerous, there was always a gratifying sense of challenge and accomplishment that provided meaning, a deep level of enjoyment (often after the fact), and even a sense of euphoria or ecstasy.

Curiously, Flow was almost never found in leisure activities such as going to the spa, drinking alcohol, consuming the privileges of wealth or watching TV. Actually, one *can* vicariously experience Flow by watching someone else performing in a state of Flow—it's just a not as meaningful, enduring or mind altering. One can experience appreciation, joy and wonder seeing 2 people in love, but will never come close to having the depth and intensity of experience that the 2 lovers are having.

"Being your best means learning how to create Flow in your life and in your relationship."

As touched on earlier, we are enamored with excellence. We love watching the best musicians, artists, actors, athletes and even lovers performing in the zone, demonstrating a level of excellence that is both inspiring and humbling. Yet, most of us are content being spectators. And because of this, we settle for a life, or marriage, that falls short of what anyone might define as a peak experience. The secret to living a life and having a marriage full of peak experiences isn't to be the best, but to be *your* best. Being *your* best means learning how to create Flow in your life and in your relationship.

What is FLOW and how do we access it?

Flow is what makes life worth living. A Flow experience is so rich and gratifying that people will engage in the activity for the sheer sake of doing it, with little to no concern for getting anything out of it. And when we've completed the activity, we feel changed in some small or even profound way. We sense that we have grown, evolved or developed more complexity as a result.

A pianist in Flow plays for the sheer love and satisfaction of playing, not for a paycheck at the end of the night. A kayaker in Flow paddles the rapids, drops and eddies of a river to experience the challenge, exhilaration and oneness of being in the river, not to get from point A to point B. Two passionate lovers in the thralls of sexual union aren't in it for the orgasms waiting for them at the end, although that's part of it. They're in it because there is nothing they'd rather be doing in that moment. A sexual climax *is* pleasurable, however, it's not always a rich or meaningful experience. Pleasure is a superficial experience that can be had without any effort on your part. True enjoyment requires focus, psychic investment, forward movement, and somehow in the end leaves you feeling changed.

Besides all being Flow experiences, the preceding 3 scenarios have 2 things in common. First, depending on the activity and the amount of challenge or risk associated with it, they all, to varying degrees, induce the release of chemicals that make you feel good, tighten your focus, and leave you wanting more. They all have a bliss factor. Sounds kind of like falling in love, doesn't it? The second thing the individuals in these scenarios all share is the ability to control their inner experience, and when you control your inner experience, you're able to determine the quality of your life.

As you've probably already experienced, controlling your inner experience is more challenging when another person you care about is involved. This is the true test of how grounded you are—you make your own reality and the whims and moods of another don't affect you.

One gift we've given to each other is the conscious effort that during the roughest experiences, we don't allow it to affect our states at the same time. If one of us is struggling, the other steps up to the plate to help elevate the other's mood— change the meaning, change the situation and remind us what's most important.

In other words, the euphoria of experiencing Flow is something that we can learn to manifest intentionally. And every time we experience it, we become a little more differentiated, a little more complex, a little *less* predictable, and little more interesting.

Hmmm! Are we about to "hack" the so-called "transitory state" of falling in love? You're darn right we are! If you're not feeling ready for this, just shelve the book and let it collect some dust. No harm done. It'll find its way back into your life when the time is right.

In *Flow*, Mihaly Csikszentmihalyi described a common set of almost formulaic characteristics that he observed in anyone experiencing a Flow state. As you read through each of these characteristics below, notice how many of them corroborate with your own experience of being in a state of deep enjoyment. They are not stated in any particular order of importance or syntax, nor do all of them have to be present simultaneously to be in a Flow state, however, most of them usually are. Sometimes the richness of the experience reveals itself contemplatively after the activity is over.

The first characteristic is the presence of clear goals. Whether it be baking a delectable chocolate croissant, playing a difficult guitar piece, closing a big business deal or completing a triathlon, there is always an objective that instigates the activity. As one old, motivational speaker used to say, "[Clear goals get you to move] from where you is to where you ain't."

The second is that you are completely present, entirely in the here and now. Neither the past nor the future are a part of your awareness. Truly being in the moment is a hallmark of any rich and enjoyable experience as anyone can attest.

The third characteristic of Flow is the presence of challenge and a skill set to meet the challenge. Without the presence of challenge, even the most pleasurable activities are devoid of any real meaning, deep enjoyment or compelling reason to continue them. Playing tennis against an "unworthy" opponent does not set one up for Flow. Winning a match against someone who doesn't challenge you to be your best may boost a fragile ego, but will never provide you with a rewarding experience. That said, not having the skills to challenge an opponent will likely lead to frustration and undue stress.

Directly tied to having a well-balanced challenge/skill ratio is the next Flow component and that is the presence of a built-in feedback system that immediately lets you know how you are doing in real time. In other words, within a Flow activity, it's easy to know if you're performing well, or not. Does a surgeon know if they're putting on a good performance? Does a sky-diver know if she pulled off a successful jump? Does a lover know if their counterpart is responding favorably to their presence and their touch? The sky-diver, for example, may experience a feedback sequence that moves them through a progression of chemical-inducing emotions that include fear, exhilaration, euphoria, relief, and finally joy.

The next component of a Flow experience is the presence of rules or parameters within which one must operate. Whether playing piano, chess, the stock market or racing in Le Tour de France, there will be rules and boundaries within which one must operate to have a deep sense of enjoyment. If there were no rules, no boundaries to the field and you could handle the ball anyway you wanted, any field sport would lose its attraction entirely.

The sixth aspect of Flow is concentrated focus. When you are fully present and engaged in a single activity, it's as if nothing else exists in that moment. Our ability to thoroughly enjoy anything is greatly diminished when we are distracted or our attention is divided. A handy tip to remember is that Flow follows focus.

The seventh characteristic of Flow reveals itself in a loss of self-consciousness. When the ego falls away and it's not about me-me-me anymore, you get out of your head, and merge with others and your environment in a powerful way. Remember how falling in love has been likened to being out of one's mind? Something to think about.

When I interact with my husband I do my best to speak to him from my heart, from a place of love, understanding and compassion. When we come from a place of frustration or anger we are no longer supporting and uplifting the other.

The final component of Flow is a distorted sense of time. When one is fully engaged in a rich and/or enjoyable experience, one's sense of time is warped to either feel extremely compressed or sometimes even stretched out.

FLOW and Being in Love

All 8 of these Flow characteristics show up consistently in a passionate life-long love affair. If you want to fall in love over and over again with your mate, simply (easy for me to say!) learn how to consistently be in flow with them. After all, Flow was the state you were experiencing when you fell in love in the first place. Let's go back in our minds together to when we felt ecstatic just to be sitting down across the table from our potential life partners and see how Flow's characteristics show up in full force.

All love affairs are not without the presence of clear goals or we wouldn't be in them. Two other words for goal are the nouns *want* and *desire*. We desire love and connection (one of the 7 core needs); we want companionship; we desire sex; we want to feel significant; we want to feel wanted; we want the person we are in love with to reciprocate; we don't want to lose the person we are in love with; maybe we want the security of having someone else take care of us; perhaps we want to form an economic alliance, and the list can go on and on.

Next, when we are with someone that we are falling in love with or in love with, we are fully present.

To be fully present with your spouse and your kids is the biggest gift you can give them and, in my opinion, the lack of it is one of the biggest culprits to a deteriorating relationship. When you're present, you have the greatest opportunity to understand your mate; to see their subtle cues; their body language so you can translate their full message; they feel that you care, encouraging them to open up to you more fully and deeply.

In addition, it gives you the greatest opportunity to reduce misunderstandings. Think about how much you enjoy talking to someone who is genuinely interested in what you're saying and is at full attention. For me, it's one of the best gifts I receive and can give. Conversely, how frustrating it feels to not be heard.

When you are doing what you want to be doing and being with the one you want to be with, you are always in the moment, right in the here and now and nothing else matters. The rest of the world disappears. That's because your focus is concentrated on that person. It's as if you have blinders on. You're so absorbed in each other that your awareness of what's going on around you drops off precipitously. If the love affair is one-sided, your obsession can be so focused that it's difficult to think about anything else. This focus and presence alters your sense of time. An hour can feel like an eternity or 3 hours like 5 minutes.

Whether you are trying to get someone's attention, dating someone you are extremely attracted or magnetized to, or in the thralls of a passionate love affair, you are consistently challenged in ways that compel you to perform at your very best.

Once we get married, we can grow to dislike these challenges. We feel that our life is complicated enough and want easy sailing. So we bite our tongue to not rock the boat, or we express our frustration with anger. Instead, we need to embrace these differences; they make life interesting, thought provoking, and open up a world that we wouldn't see without another person suggesting a different point of view. So much of how we feel about a situation can be changed in an instant by a change in perspective.

When you want something bad enough, you stretch yourself beyond your normal limits in order to secure the object of your desire, your goal. When you are falling in love or in a love affair, the person you want has mystery; they're not a foregone conclusion. When you have them, it's only for that moment and you know that. They are always just barely within your reach, pushing you to do whatever it takes to close the gap. It keeps you on your toes and inspires you to consistently take your game to a new level. And just when you think you've got them figured out, they throw you a curveball.

When people are young, they haven't even really figured out who they are yet. As people get older, they are often afraid to let you see who they are and vice versa. So as the dance continues, the feedback loop is continuous. Whether you're just falling-in-love or in the clutches of a volatile love affair, you know day by day, hour by hour and sometimes minute by minute how well you are doing and what the state of affairs is. If you are mindful, you can regulate your actions in real time to stay on course with reaching your objective.

Unfortunately, so many women, because of past hurts and score keeping, won't give their husband positive feedback when he's trying to please them or making an effort to improve their marriage. This is one of the worst things you can do to your mate and your relationship. When one of you makes an effort, the other needs to acknowledge it in a way that gives them positive feedback. If you set it up so your mate can't win no matter what they do, the value of the feedback loop is diminished and in most cases your spouse will stop trying to please you, altogether.

All the while, there are always certain unspoken rules of the game that must be adhered to. These rules are often in the form of a code of conduct that demonstrates to the other person the quality of one's honor, respect and loyalty. For example, if one is truly in love with the other, they will restrict their romantic and sexual behaviors to that person rather than playing the field, so to speak. Another behavioral code might be that a man who truly wants a woman will express intentions to marry her rather than leave their relationship open-ended. It's nearly impossible to stay in love without demonstrating that you are choosing each other within the parameters of a committed relationship (marriage).

And finally, when you are in-love, there is a loss of self-consciousness. Whether you're a teacher standing in front of a classroom, a performer on stage, hosting a dinner party or a lover playing their partner like an instrument, if you are self-conscious about what you are doing, you will feel stress, anxiety and apprehension—none of which induce Flow. When you are in love, your separateness diminishes and your ego gets out of the way of your desire to merge with the other person. You lose self-consciousness while giving your best. This isn't to say that you stop paying close attention to how you look or act. But instead of coming from a place of self-consciousness, it's coming from the desire to be your best.

You're not worried about how you look or what someone is going to think. When your self-consciousness disappears, it's not about you anymore. It's about the blending of energies that make us.

"When you are in love, your separateness diminishes and your ego gets out of the way of your desire to merge with the other person."

Wow! Need I say more? Do you see in this the built-in recipe for a powerful, chemical-cocktail high? All you've got to do is keep doing what you did in the beginning and you'll get the same result, right? Well, it's not that simple but it sure gives insight into where we went wrong in our relationships. And that's the good news. Herein lies the magic, wonder and even genius behind marriage.

"In order for us to consistently reproduce the euphoria of falling in love with our mates, we've got to consistently grow ourselves in body, mind and spirit."

In order for us to consistently reproduce the euphoria of falling in love with our mates, we've got to consistently grow ourselves in body, mind and spirit. It's as if God gave us the experience of falling-in-love as bait, as an appetizer, as an inducement to lure us into the University of Marital Bliss. This is where we get an advanced degree in driving the Ferrari we've had sitting under the old, dusty tarp in our garage.

For a minute, let's go back and look at the 8 characteristics of Flow as just presented in the context of falling in love. If these 8 characteristics were to comprise a formula, which ones are obviously missing in your relationship? I would bet that you can identify at least 3, if not 4 or 5. When you do this, it's not hard to see why you may have lost that lovin' feeling or at least the passion you may have once had. So, if falling in love all over again is as simple as getting into Flow with your mate, how do we get back into Flow? Well now that you understand the characteristics of flow, let's talk about the Conditions of Flow.

The Conditions of Flow

The 8 characteristics of Flow discussed are really all the hallmarks of being in Flow. They are Flow's symptoms if you will. However, to produce a rich, ecstatic, "flowy" experience, there are 3 things that set you up for it as pointed out by Steven Kotler in his book, *The Rise of Superman*. Whether you are a mother nursing a newborn baby, an investor setting up a creative real estate transaction or a lover introducing a new form of sex-play into the bedroom, there are 3 conditions that trigger flow:

1. the presence of *clear goals* or objectives,
2. an *optimal challenge to skill ratio*, and
3. an automatic, *built-in feedback system*.

These 3 things give you focus, they put you in the here-and-now, compel you to perform your best, give you the opportunity to make real time tweaks, and set you up for a natural chemical high. When you face a compelling challenge and have the tools to tackle it, your body gives you progressive little squirts of norepinephrine which tighten your focus and bring all your available resources to bear to take on the challenge. When you get feedback that your actions are moving you in the direction of your goals, your body releases dopamine into your system which serves to not just make you feel good, but also enhance your ability to make further creative distinctions and insights. The here-and-now focus of Flow enhances our decision-making ability.

The fears that would normally stand in the way of our progress toward our goals seem to diminish because we've gotten out of our ego and started focusing more on the other person and their needs. When we do this, our self-doubts and insecurities evaporate because we're not thinking about me-me-me. When we reach this timeless state, we are living in the moment. The past is, well, the past, and the future doesn't exist because it's the future. When you are fully engaged and performing your best in the now, there is no pain or emotional baggage. And the feedback you are getting, assuming it's favorable, sets you up for a chemical blast that keeps you wanting more. Now, if we just keep doing what we're doing, our ability to maintain or recreate the experience snowballs, because we've created an environment that reinforces itself. In other words, the more you do it, the more you want to do it.

Flow is a way to transcend your present reality, whatever that is, and move forward with the best version of yourself. Because when you are in flow, you are your best version of yourself—you've got your A game on. And the sensations, emotions and positive reinforcement you get when you're in this zone are addictive. The possibility of getting more keeps you coming back for more. Another way of relating this is to say that when something or someone consistently makes us feel good, we develop a positive association to them in our nervous system, which causes us to think about, plan for and anticipate similar results in the future. Our motivation to be with someone, attract that someone, please that someone, and meet that someone's needs at a high level goes through the ceiling when our experience is always good.

As a couple, why don't we do this? Maybe a better question is, why did we stop doing this? By now, we can all easily answer the question. We lost our focus, we never set clear goals for our marriage and we haven't fostered an environment of challenge or skill development (personal growth) to meet the challenge. Why did this happen? Life happened. We started getting complacent and taking each other for granted the second we got married. We treated marriage (the act of getting married) as a jumping off point for the rest of our life. Kind of like, "Now that that's done, we can get on with our life". We defocused on each other and turned our attention to our careers, raising children, and acquiring the next "trophy" to help rationalize the hard work and sacrifices we are making by defocusing on our marriage. Ironic, huh?

Recreating Love using FLOW

So, how do we get back into Flow and create the conditions for falling in love again? First, you need to get clear on what you want out of your marriage.

Hopefully you did that in the last chapter. This refocuses your attention on your marriage and your mate. Flow follows focus, and in particular, focus on something that has consequences. I can't think of anything that has more consequences than your marriage.

Next, you've got to introduce challenge and growth. When there is significant challenge or even risk associated with an activity, the opportunity for the release of the euphoria-inducing cocktail of dopamine, norepinephrine, endorphins and anandamide grows precipitously.

So how do we introduce challenge and a healthy dose of risk into our relationship without compromising it? Well, first let's take a look at the role that risk played when we were dating. For some, dating is a high-stakes game. I mean you are really putting yourself out there. The dating scene is fraught with risk at every turn, and talk about vulnerability! The fact is, the only way that we can experience deep connection with another human being is by putting ourselves out there, risking rejection, criticism and humiliation.

But what happens when we put our best foot forward, lay it all on the line, and the other person responds favorably? What happens when we give a little love that we're not certain will be reciprocated and we actually get a little love back? We then stretch our neck out a little farther, and then a little farther, and then a little farther. Why do we do this? Because every time we risk ourselves for love and connection, and get a little more of what we are seeking, we get little shots of dopamine. And once a pattern of behavior is established that is consistently rewarded by a cocktail high of love, excitement, ecstasy and bonding, the process self-perpetuates until something breaks the pattern.

The question is, how do we introduce a healthy level of challenge and risk into our relationship, and still have the certainty and security that should be inherent in a marriage? The short answer is that we each continue to grow and evolve ourselves mentally, spiritually and even physically. In other words, we become a story being written in real time; an unfolding yet evolving mystery to be observed and solved by our mate. That's what our mate was to us in the beginning and us to them. It's one of the things that induced the focus, clear objectives and skill application that put us into Flow.

Both the challenge and skill components of Flow are equally important, and they will be the primary focus of the rest of this chapter. To consistently produce the level of Flow that will induce you and your partner to fall in love with each other over and over again, you will each need to learn to provide a healthy level of challenge to your relationship, while simultaneously growing yourselves to meet the challenges provided by your mate. This boils down to one thing: constant and never-ending personal growth. Your own growth turns you into an unfolding mystery and your mate's growth compels you to grow to meet the challenges associated with being intimate with someone who is a slowly moving target. The next diagram below illustrates how this works.

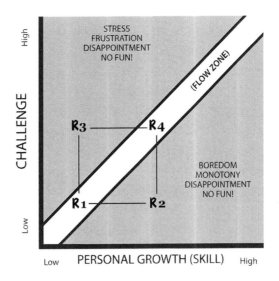

FLOW- A GRAPHIC ILLUSTRATION

I'm borrowing this concept from Professor Csikszentmihalyi's book, *Flow*, because it is the simplest example I can think of to illustrate the relationship between challenge and skill as it pertains to Flow. Let's use tennis as an example of a potential Flow activity with Rafa, a man learning to play tennis. You'll notice that the diagram is a chart with 2 axes; "Challenge" on one axis and "Skill" on the other. The letter **R** on the chart represents Rafa and you'll notice 4 different points on the chart that Rafa has the potential of experiencing. In fact, there are infinite points on the chart that Rafa could experience but for the sake of this example, we will use just 4.

When Rafa first starts out learning tennis (position **R1**), his skill is very low, but the challenge is also very low. All he has to do is make contact with the ball, hit it over the net, and he's feeling good. Even as a beginner, Rafa can be in Flow because just having the racket in his hands and hitting balls is a new and exciting experience for him.

However, for Rafa to stay in Flow he must continue to increase the challenges he faces playing tennis, while simultaneously increasing his skills to meet those challenges. This might mean that while he's taking lessons, he is presented with new and more difficult skill sets to learn. However, mastering a skill is not by itself rewarding unless there is an application of the skill where one can experience a sense of competence and accomplishment. So as Rafa continues to advance in his tennis game, he will require playing partners that challenge and inspire him.

If Rafa is at position **R2**, he has advanced in his skills beyond that of his playing partners, or is ready to expand his skill set to a new level. He is bored, uninspired, and in danger of losing interest in tennis. At this point Rafa has a few options. He can quit tennis and look for another activity that keeps him engaged, but that will rob him of his opportunity for personal growth and mastery. He can increase the challenge by either finding more worthy opponents, or he can inspire his playing partners to practice and grow their skills to a new level by continuing to practice and learn.

If Rafa is at point **R3**, he is in over his head. His playing partners are much too experienced, and he is frustrated and not having fun. His opponents' serves are just too fast and his rudimentary ball hitting skills are no match for the lobs, drop shots, and cross court backhands he's getting. What can he do to get back into Flow and reinforce his love for tennis? He can either start working harder on his game by taking lessons, getting a coach and practicing, or he can seek out players that are more at his level. If Rafa does the latter, he takes the risk of never growing his skills, getting bored, and eventually losing his zeal for the game. The best thing Rafa can do is grow himself into a better player.

If Rafa is at point **R4**, he is in Flow and his experience playing tennis is very rewarding. The challenge and excitement of playing against more advanced players has rewarded the hard work he has put in growing his skills and his physical fitness level. To maintain this high level of Flow, Rafa must either continue to practice or continue to grow his level of fitness, or both. He might join a tennis league and start playing competitively, or broaden his game by taking up doubles playing which has a whole new and exciting dynamic.

Notice the relationship between skill and challenge. When the skill is roughly equal to the challenge, it puts you in the Flow Channel. If the challenge is too much, you experience anxiety, frustration, fear and stress. If the challenge is too low relative to your skill level, you experience boredom and a different kind of frustration. To stay in Flow, your challenge must continue to grow along with your skill set to meet the challenge. As Rafa moves from position **R1** in the direction of position **R4** and beyond, the challenges he faces increase in complexity, as do the skills he develops to face them. As long as Rafa's challenges continue to increase along with his skills, Rafa will remain in Flow. However, if Rafa grows in skill but his tennis partners stagnate, he will either lose interest in tennis or go looking for someone to play with that he finds challenging. If Rafa's tennis partners continue to get better but he stagnates, he will lose his interest in playing with them because he finds it stressful and humiliating. For Rafa to stay in Flow, he must not only consistently grow his skills but also the challenges with which to apply those skills. Now, let's put this concept of the Flow Channel to use in our relationships.

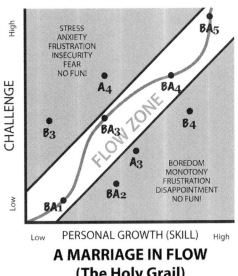

A MARRIAGE IN FLOW
(The Holy Grail)

Study "The Holy Grail" diagram for a minute and then use it to follow along with the example of Brad and Angelina, where you'll see the dynamic relationship between *challenge* and *skill,* and how it keeps you in Flow as a couple. Note: Any parallels to anyone you might know or know of, are purely coincidental.

Brad and Angelina fell in love because they were intrigued with each other. Their masculine and feminine essences were polarizing and the animal attraction was magnified by the sense of feeling that each had met their match. Remember how Dr. David Schnarch suggested that we are attracted to someone with a similar level of differentiation? Well, we're also attracted to our equals in appearance and intelligence. When someone is similar to us in intelligence, education, athletic prowess and values, we can find them to be, both a worthy quest, and still within our reach. When we feel challenged by someone who we are magnetized to, our propensity to rise to the challenge is heightened because we sense that we've got what it takes to meet whatever test comes our way. We have a strong desire to solve the mystery, see behind the curtain, or maybe just spar with them a little. And when we are rewarded for that effort with a favorable outcome, we get a little shot of dopamine, anandamide and maybe some endorphins, which polarize and magnetize us even more. At that point, we might go to new and great lengths to keep having the experience.

At the beginning of their relationship, Brad and Angelina (B&A) are at point **BA1** on the diagram. They are in Flow. Remember, Flow is the condition when the challenge in the relationship is roughly in balance with the skill required to meet the challenge. For the time being, the inherent uncertainty, novelty, variety and mystery of being in a new relationship provides all the challenge B&A need to stay focused on each other, stay in the moment with each other, stay tuned in to each other, keep working to anticipate each other's needs, and all the while perform at their best. B&A also enjoy the fact that they both love a good cheeseburger with onion rings and a cold beer.

But nothing stays static. No one can stay in Flow (in love in this case) without increased challenge, any more than anyone can stay in Flow by remaining in high school his or her whole life, as appealing as that may seem to some. The fact is, if neither Brad nor Angelina continues to grow and evolve themselves, the allure of their relationship will fade over time. As exciting and attractive as someone's attributes may have been at the beginning of a love affair, if they don't *continue* to be exciting and attractive, they will lose their appeal. No one really cares what you did or who you were in the past. All that matters is what you do now, who you are now, and who you are becoming.

Back to Brad and Angelina. If they are at point **BA2**, one or both of them have needs that are not being met. Maybe one or both have become complacent since the chemical cocktail of falling in love has worn off. Maybe Brad is a foregone conclusion and doesn't excite Angelina the way he used to. Or perhaps Angelina stopped dolling herself up for him and he's lost the anticipation of seeing her every morning. What has to happen to get them back into Flow? In the first instance, Brad needs to re-engage Angelina's interest and curiosity by growing himself in some way. He might take up a new hobby, take his diet or fitness level up a notch, collaborate with her to do something she's always wanted to but he was never in support of, or maybe start pursuing her like he did in the beginning. In each instance, Brad and Angelina both need to be more of the person that their mate deserves; more of the person that attracts the kind of person they want in their life.

So what happens if Angelina takes an interest in health and well-being, becomes convicted to eat a vegan diet, and starts meditating every morning before breakfast? Well, if Brad doesn't demonstrate a willingness to entertain and engage with Angelina in her newfound practices, he will end up in position **B3**, she'll be in position **A3**, and neither will be in Flow with each other. Brad will feel like she isn't the girl he fell in love with, and perhaps feel a real or imagined separation growing between them. Angelina will feel like Brad isn't mindful of his health which she interprets as a lack of caring for their future as a couple. If Brad doesn't use Angelina's new passion for health to spur him on to new horizons, Angelina may find Brad's lack of mindfulness discouraging and unattractive. Brad has 3 choices:

1. He can do nothing and keep himself at position **B3** in which case they both will experience anxiety, frustration and possible stress,
2. He can expand himself and join Angelina in exploring her new convictions in which case they'll be in position **BA3** or,
3. Brad may grow his level of differentiation to where he simply honors and respects whatever new convictions Angelina brings to the table. Either way, Brad is growing himself to stay in connection with Angelina

(position **BA3**), and as a result they stay in Flow because they are both moving forward with focus, engagement, and personal growth.

Now, Brad wants to take the quality of their lives to a new level, so he invites Angelina to go with him to a personal development seminar. Angelina has seen some of these advertised on Google and Facebook and thinks they're a bunch of hype. In truth, she's quite content with the way things are and is not very motivated to listen to a personal development evangelist. So Brad goes alone.

After 3 days of paradigm-shifting ideas and personal breakthroughs, Brad feels like he has a new lease on life. He's excited about the future and can't wait to start pursuing the life of his dreams. Angelina, however, doesn't share his enthusiasm. Not only does she not share in the energy and profundity of Brad's experience, but she also feels unsettled because she doesn't know the new Brad or what it means for their relationship. Angelina is now at position **A4** because the change in Brad is more than she can handle. At the same time, Brad's new energy, awareness and mindset puts him at position **B4** because, for the moment anyway, Angelina doesn't want to play ball at the new level that he desires. Both are out of Flow when it comes to their relationship.

To bring them back into Flow as a couple, Angelina either needs to stretch herself to join Brad in his new quest for a higher quality of life (position **BA4**), or Brad needs to lower his expectations, quell his enthusiasm, and settle for less than what he wants in life. The latter, however, isn't really an option because going backwards in our personal and spiritual development is emotionally and psychologically disastrous. Once one has a glimpse of new possibilities, it's hard to pretend they don't exist.

That all said, if Brad truly loves Angelina, he will continue to work on himself while exercising patience with his beloved in expectation that she will eventually integrate herself with his desires and values in a meaningful way. But this can only go on for so long before Brad yearns to experience life with a like-minded person. However, if they are both highly differentiated, they will choose to support and integrate with each other out of love, honor and respect. In order for this to happen, they would both, once again, be on an upward path of growth, pushing, pulling or inspiring each other up to a higher place. Their mutual desire to stay in Flow with each other will compel both to continually grow of their own accord, and also to stretch themselves to stay integrated and in meaningful connection with the other.

In the final scenario, Brad and Angelina really love each other but feel like the life is gone from their relationship. They both want something more and realize that if they can't reignite the passion (i.e., get back into Flow together) their 17-year marriage may be over. So they collaborate and decide to go to a marriage mastery retreat together? If possible, they both want to take their relationship to new heights and eliminate any pain, frustration and baggage that might be preventing them from having an extraordinary marriage. They both agree to play full out at the workshop even if it means going places that have been off-limits before. Just the thought of doing this together puts them in Flow. The workshop proves to be really fun, very challenging, amazingly paradigm shifting, and profoundly life changing. After the event, Brad and Angelina find themselves in an amazing state of Flow because they see each other with new eyes, are excited about the prospect of their future together, and are having mind-blowing sex for the first time in years. Brad and Angelina are now at position **BA5**. They are in Flow and at a higher level than ever before.

Interestingly, none of these positions on the Flow diagram are stable, meaning that there is no point where things will simply stay the same if Brad and Angelina do nothing. To get into Flow at any given time, one or both of them need to be growing, stretching or expanding themselves. To stay in Flow at any given time, both of them need to work together as a team to reach ever-increasing new heights of experience. Just as a rock-climbing team will often switch leads, sometimes inspiring each other, other times pushing or pulling each other, and once in a while saving each other; so it is in a marriage. The joy is in meeting the challenges presented when 2 evolving and differentiated adults choose to share their life together. If you're saying to yourself that this isn't the way marriage is supposed to be, you're forgetting that marriage isn't just about being married. It's the ultimate incubator for personal development, and the realization of your highest and best self.

This may sound daunting, but it isn't. Everything we've talked about in this entire book sets you up to have this experience. Everything from adopting a new and profound paradigm for your marriage; growing in your capacity to love; keeping your vows at a deeper level; meeting your mate's 7 core needs;

nurturing your polar differences; chasing your mate like a prize worth having; setting higher standards for yourself; taking your physical and spiritual self to new levels; growing in your differentiation; to even creating a vision for your marriage. Each of these things by themselves promote and evidence personal growth. In other words, if each of you is expanding your capacity to love; daily keeping your explicit and implicit vows; meeting your mate's needs at a high level; nurturing the masculine or feminine attributes that attracted you to each other in the first place; pursuing your mate like you did in the beginning; growing and expanding your philosophical and spiritual paradigms; and growing in your own unique sense of self, you will each be growing like weeds. Your marriage will be dynamic, exciting, meaningful and fulfilling. Your marriage will be in Flow.

If you want to experience *Ecstatic* Flow (the bliss and euphoria of falling in love) the fastest way is to inject your Flow experience with *risk* and *novelty*. In other words, you need to break your routines and start sailing a little towards the edge of the world. I know, I know, we love routine. In fact, we thrive on it, depend on it, and rely on it. We have morning routines, bedtime routines, meal routines, and even sex routines. They give us certainty and predictability in an uncertain world. But, routine is boring and uninspiring. In fact, it can be downright stagnating and any good personal trainer will attest to this. Even your muscles will stop responding to your efforts if you keep doing the same thing you've always done. Doing what you've done to get where you are will never get you where you want to go.

"Doing what you've done to get where you are will never get you where you want to go."

In his book *In Over Our Heads*, Harvard psychologist Robert Kegan, explains how sameness promotes stagnation and entropy, while things like diversity, variety and risk are an optimal environment for personal development. Remember that certainty is a foundational component of a good marriage, but *uncertainty* is a requirement of a passionate, blissful marriage.

Risk taking and its accompanying uncertainty make us feel alive, as does the experience of novelty. As Steven Kotler pointed out in *The Rise of Superman*, extreme sports have the ability to induce an ecstatic Flow state with shocking speed because they get us acutely focused, they get us super present, they take everything we've got to do them well, and they provide immediate feedback as to how well we are doing (i.e., we come out alive). Anyone who has skydived, base jumped, ridden a big wave, or pulled off a back flip on a snowboard can attest to this. They all experience Flow at an extreme level—they feel alive, they feel bliss.

In the context of marriage, some have found ways to meet this extreme risk/reward quotient by sleeping around, having extra-marital affairs, swinging, or engaging in sexually deviant behaviors. All these activities meet needs for variety, uncertainty, and "feeling alive" possibly not being met in the context of one's marriage. However, they do not, for the most part, support a healthy, long-term love affair. For many, just having a good marriage isn't good enough. They want to feel alive. They want to want, and have the validation of being wanted. They want the rush of falling in love.

So the question is, how *do* we introduce uncertainty, novelty and risk into an environment that is supposed to be inherently

> **"For many, just having a good marriage isn't good enough. They want to feel alive."**

safe and certain? Well, we do it by pushing ourselves to the limits and boundaries of the marriage playing field. Uncertainty, novelty and risk add complexity to our relationship, and complexity requires us to rise to new challenges, without which we would die of complacency, boredom and spiritual infancy.

There are endless ways to introduce adventure, excitement, variety, humor and novelty into your home, your romantic life, your sex life, your social life, and even your kitchen life.

Novelty and unpredictability can come from mixing up your routines, driving different routes, swapping who does what in the house, preparing new or exotic cuisine, going to social events that you would typically avoid, exploring alternative spiritual paths, listening to new music genres, engaging in new hobbies (e.g., skydiving or beekeeping), learning new skill sets, rearranging your house, reinventing your wardrobe, training for a triathlon, or saying yes to things you've always said no to.

You can introduce risk by getting a tattoo, switching careers, telling your spouse something they don't know about you, changing your life-long hairstyle, hanging a sex swing in your basement, or trying something new in the bedroom that was previously off limits for you. When stacked on top of your "everyday" Flow experience, each of these things could refocus your attention, get you in the here-and-now, give you new objectives to strive for, massively stimulate your personal growth, and give you feedback that injects you with a refreshing chemical cocktail of *Love Potion #9.*

The questions are: How creative can you get? How loving? How adventurous? How innovative? How thoughtful? How romantic? How mysterious? How provocative? How crazy? How present? And how to do it all in the context of your marriage? How do we keep growing ourselves for the sake of keeping our mate engaged, intrigued and magnetized? How do we keep up with a mate who is on an upward path of realizing his or her own human potential?

The answer is that we grow. We grow by expanding ourselves, by familiarizing and investing ourselves in our mate's desires and dreams, and by collaborating with them on their fulfillment. A few activities we enjoy that create an environment for us to grow together are attending seminars, workshops, reading books independently that we discuss, dynamic conversations, setting health and fitness goals, and taking action together to achieve these results.

The other answer, however, is that we've got to get out of our heads. As Americans, we can be obsessed with this, going to great lengths and spending fortunes to still or drown out the myriad of voices in our minds. These voices come from our cerebral sense of self that's always asking, "Am I good enough, smart enough, worthy enough?" "Is she good enough, sexy enough, motherly enough or Catholic enough?" We are haunted by voices of the past and anxious about the hypothetical and fictitious future—about what could, should or might happen. These voices cause us anxiety, stress us out, induce depression, cause frustration and discontent, and can make us feel inadequate or hopeless. We go to extremes to drown out these voices by listening to music, watching movies, drinking alcohol, taking drugs, meditating, praying, doing yoga, watching sports, taking physical risks, and even causing ourselves physical pain.

However, when we are in the euphoric state of falling in love, our self sort of dissolves and merges with our beloved. We stop focusing on ourselves, stop worrying about the past or future, and start acting for the greater good of the relationship. Our energy combines in a synergistic way that makes you feel like the two of you together are greater than the sum of your parts. Interestingly, the little flaws, quirks and idiosyncrasies that later become sources of upset and frustration, were likely always there, you just didn't care because you weren't focusing on them, analyzing them, or assigning any meaning to them. Why? Because, you were out of your head, and in your heart and spirit! When you are "in love", the ego falls away and you stop thinking about yourself. It's not about me-me-me anymore. Your focus becomes more about what you can do to love, honor, attract, and capture the attention of your beloved. You are given a glimpse of what life is like when you grow your *self* up.

Why then, you might ask, are we willing to put so much energy and resources into getting out of our heads yet stay in our heads when it comes to our marriages? My answer is that we gravitate toward "mind-less" or "mind-full" (in the sense of filling our minds) activities that offer quick relief from our suffering, without having to make a large personal commitment. The problem is, these activities don't usually provide any impetus for personal growth.

Marriage is the only environment that I know of that provides a perpetually compelling reason for personal growth, has a built-in feedback system, and offers an unending reward of love and connection, an amazing sense of significance, a deep well of meaning and fulfillment, and an always-open refreshment stand serving up tropical concoctions of ecstasy, euphoria and bliss. The price for access however, is a hunger, thirst and commitment to grow your "self" as a human and spiritual being.

Part 2 – Spiritual development (short and sweet)

The second and most magical part of our perpetual love potion happens when we transcend our conventional sense of self with the understanding that we are truly divine beings having a human experience. When you reach this higher level of consciousness, you see your mate with new eyes. It continually and spontaneously dawns on you how miraculously and wonderfully made they are. When this happens, you see them with a continually renewed freshness.

In his new song *Fresh Eyes*, Andy Grammer uniquely conveys this experience when he croons the words, *"I got these fresh eyes, never seen you before like this. My God, you're beautiful. It's like the first time when we open the door, before we got used to usual."* It reminds me again of the *"Piña Colada Song"* by Rupert Holmes where he tells the story of a couple experiencing the marriage doldrums. Remember in the song, she places a personal ad looking for a man who shares her thirst for living. The kicker is that her husband is the one who responds to the ad. What makes the song so poignant is that the qualities that they were each looking for in a *new* person, they already had in each other. They had just taken each other for granted and underappreciated each other. It took a crisis for them to realize that what they wanted, they already had. What this crisis gave them was a fresh set of eyes.

When you learn to get really present with your mate and begin to view them with new eyes, their beauty magnifies, and their attributes that complement and attract you to them become highlighted. When you begin to not only turn off but live without judgment, criticism, analysis, and the need to make sense of things, and grow into love, acceptance, non-judgment, and allowing—it will be as if you've donned rose-tinted glasses that airbrush your world with an ethereal glow.

Eastern philosophies teach the concept of "mindfulness". Mindfulness is about being fully present and eliminating distraction. It's bringing all your attention to what it is you're engaged in, with an ever-expanding insight that puts the mundane and trivial distractions of life in perspective. In other words, you could say that mindfulness is the state of keeping the main thing *the main thing*. In a fully present and mindful state, in which one exists at a well-differentiated level of consciousness, all the trivia in your marriage that taints your perception of your mate, and is cause for frustration and pain just seems to vaporize. The complexity diminishes and what once felt difficult becomes effortlessly blissful.

When you learn to regulate the dynamic of Flow in your relationship and do it with mindfulness, consciousness and fresh eyes, you have the formula for a life-long, passionate love affair.

Well, there you have it! I've almost run out of things to say. However, I will say this. Don't take any of this too seriously. As much as I would like to give you a plug-and-play formula to follow, marriage is not a mathematical equation. It's more a matter of the heart and spirit. It's fluid—kind of like the ocean, kind of like a woman, full of surprises and challenges at every turn.

While the principles shared in this book are tried and true, their application requires intuition, finesse and artistry. I like to use the analogy of landing an airplane because although you can teach one how to do it from a book, the application of the theory requires focus, presence, sensitivity and lots of practice. Practice is something you do consistently and make a part of your daily life.

Now, give yourself the gift of continued learning and support by joining our online community at www.GreatMarriageGreatLife.com. Kimberly and I share our own real-time challenges, solutions, insights and excitement through our weekly blog and keep you updated on our latest programs and events. Nothing has changed our lives for the better more than attending events with other like-minded people who refuse to settle for mediocrity, and want to live their lives at a more profound level. We hope to see you at one of ours.

ACTION STEPS

1. Start meeting the challenges in your relationship with personal growth that will equip you to better meet the challenge.

2. Identify 3 areas of pain or frustration that would significantly benefit from your own personal development, e.g., letting go the need to be right; overcoming your alcoholism; stopping the destructive act of withholding love or sex as a manipulation; meeting your mate's need for communication even if you don't feel like you benefit from it, etc.

3. Think of 3 ways that you can grow and expand yourself that could be exciting or intriguing to your mate. Take immediate action to buy the book, sign yourself up, schedule the event, take the class, or whatever. Do it now! There is no tomorrow! A decision is no decision at all if you don't take action on it.

4. For immediate results, take action toward doing some novel, risky or challenging things that are in your comfort wheelhouse but maybe you've just put off or neglected. In other words, start doing what you know to do but have just forgotten or made excuses not to do.

5. Help us turn this message into a mass movement of change. We really believe that the future we all want begins in our own homes with our relationships. You can help us by telling your friends about this book, writing us a review on Amazon or getting involved with our community at www.GreatMarriageGreatLife.com. That all said, the biggest contribution you can make is to live the message.

FINDING YOUR 20%

I'M BACK! I JUST couldn't help but think you might be feeling overwhelmed right now so I'm going to throw you a lifesaver. One of the things I've learned in life is that the most profound results often come from the simplest things. It goes back to the Pareto Principle or the 80/20 rule. Eighty percent of your results are going to come from 20% of your efforts. It's up to you to identify the 20% that will give you the 80% you desire.

The 20% is self-evident when you really stop and get mindful about it. It may be as simple as doing what you did in the beginning only with strong intention, focus and consciousness. Or maybe it's simply treating your mate as a lover treats a lover. Maybe for you it's about keeping your vows, but at a new and profound level. Or, it could be nurturing the polarity in your marriage so that your masculine or feminine energies are re-ignited. Maybe the Holy Grail for you is collaborating with your mate to introduce a healthy sense of variety and excitement into your relationship. Whatever it is, when you get mindful, your gut will tell you what you need to do.

To help you out with this we've got a checklist called, *Finding My 20%* that you can download for free at www.GreatMarriageGreatLife.com. It's under RESOURCES>FORMS. *Finding My 20%* lists virtually every concept found in the book.

As you go through it, check all (and I mean, *all*) the items that you know will make a difference to the quality of love, connection, sex and passion in your relationship. After you've done that, choose the 20% (e.g., 1 of 5, 2 of 10, or 6 of 30) that you know will have the most profound impact on the love and connection you're currently feeling with your mate, the attraction you currently have for each other, and the quality and frequency of sex you're having. You know what these things are! You know what your mate craves from you that you've either ignored, been too distracted to acknowledge or just too selfish to give them. Then, next to each item, write down what you're going to do today to implement it into your life.

The secret to making the 20% profound is in making everything you do really count, giving it 100% of your focus, and putting all your intention into it. Three minutes of fully present, eye-to-eye, heart-to-heart connection before walking out the door in the morning is 100 times more meaningful than blankly staring across the table at each other at a fine restaurant for 3 hours once a week. Getting yourself in the moment with a hand-in-hand walk together rather than watching TV, gets your head in the right place and speaks volumes of your priorities. When you kiss your mate, consider memorizing their face, their scent and their texture. Whatever you do, go all-in and make it really, really count. Don't leave anything on the table. Because that which you are looking for, you probably already have. You just need fresh eyes.

ACTION STEPS

1. If you haven't already, download and complete your *Marriage Vision Template* under RESOURCES>FORMS at www.GreatMarriageGreatLife.com
2. If you haven't already, download and complete your *Finding My 20%* form at www.GreatMarriageGreatLife.com
3. Join our Blog for weekly inspiration and support.
4. Find yourself a group of like-minded people you can connect with.

PS. Remember that your marriage is the ultimate **Sanctuary, Classroom** and **Playground** all rolled up into one.

PPS. If you do nothing else, just simply **Love like Crazy, Grow like Crazy** and **Be True to Who You Are at Your Core**.

RESOURCES

Programs

FOREVER IN LOVE with Tad and Kimberly Horning. In just 8 short weeks or less, learn how to get the most out of your marriage—renew the passion, fulfillment, and connection that you once had and fall in love all over again. To learn more and sign up for this life-changing program, go to www.GreatMarriageGreatLife.com and look under Products and Programs.

Books

Relationships and Intimacy

Chapman, Gary D. *The 5 Love Languages: The Secret to Love That Lasts*, Chicago, Northfield Publishing, 2010

Deida, David. *The Way of the Superior Man*, Boulder, Sounds True, Inc., 2004

Evans, Jimmy with Martin, Frank. *Lifelong Love Affair: How to Have a Passionate and Deeply Rewarding Marriage*, Grand Rapids, Baker Books, 2012

Gorga, Melissa. *Love Italian Style: The Secrets of My Hot and Happy Marriage*, New York, St. Martin's Press, 2013

Gottman, John M. & Silver, Nan. *The Seven Principles for Making Marriage Work,* New York, Three Rivers Press, 1999

Gray, John. *Men Are from Mars, Women Are from Venus,* Harper Paperbacks, 2012

Haltzman, Scott. *The Secrets of Happily Married Men: Eight Ways to Win Your Wife's Heart Forever,* San Francisco, Jossey-Bass, 2006

Harley Jr., Willard F. *His Needs Her Needs: Building an Affair-Proof Marriage,* Grand Rapids, Fleming H. Revell, 2001

Hendrix, Harville and Hunt, Helen Lakelly. *Making Marriage Simple: 10 Truths for Changing the Relationship You Have into the One You Want,* New York, Harmony House, 2013

Horning, James T. *Winning at the Game of Wife,* New York, Morgan James Publishing, 2016

Morris, Howard J. and Lee, Jenny. *Women Are Crazy Men Are Stupid: The Simple Truth to a Complicated Relationship,* New York, Simon Spotlight Entertainment, 2009

Penner, Clifford L. & Penner, Joyce J. *The Married Guy's Guide to Great Sex: Building a Passionate, Intimate, and Fun Love Life,* Carol Stream, Tyndale House Publishers, 2017

Perel, Esther. *Mating in Captivity: Unlocking Erotic Intelligence,* London, Hodder and Stoughton, 2007

Roberts, Ted & Roberts, Diane. *SEXY Christians: The Purpose, Power, and Passion of Biblical Intimacy,* Grand Rapids, Baker Books, 2010

Schnarch, David. *Passionate Marriage: Keeping Love and Intimacy Alive in Committed Relationships,* New York, W. W. Norton and Company, 1997

Psychology and Personal Development

Csikszentmihalyi, Mihaly. *Flow,* New York, Harper Collins, 1990

Kegan, Robert. *In Over Our Heads: The Mental Demands of Modern Life,* President and Fellows of Harvard College, 1994

Kotler, Steven. *The Rise of Superman: Decoding the Science of Ultimate Human Performance,* London, Quercus Editions Ltd., 2014

Sexless Marriage

Davis, Michele Weiner. *The Sex-Starved Marriage: Boosting Your Marriage Libido: A Couple's Guide,* New York, Simon & Schuster, 2003

Schnarch, David. *Resurrecting Sex: Solving Sexual Problems & Revolutionizing Your Relationship,* New York, Harper Collins Publishers, 2002

Romance

Corn, Laura. *101 Nights of Grrreat Romance,* Park Avenue, 1996

Cronin, Stan. *How to Date your Wife,* Utah, Horizon Publishers & Distributors, Inc., 2004

Sex and Morality/Sex and Spirituality

Deida, David. *Finding God through Sex: Awakening the One of Spirit Through the Two of Flesh,* Boulder, Sounds True, Inc., 2005

Deida, David. *The Enlightened Sex Manual: Sexual Skills for the Superior Lover,* Boulder, Sounds True, 2007

Pilkington Jr., Clyde L. *Due Benevolence: A Survey of Biblical Sexuality – It Might Not Be What You Think,* Bible Student's Press, 2010

Roberts, Ted & Roberts, Diane. *Sexy Christians: The Purpose, Power, and Passion of Biblical Intimacy,* Grand Rapids, Baker Books, 2010

Sexual Fun and Technique

Corn, Laura. *101 Nights of Great Sex,* Park Avenue Pub. Inc., 2013

Chia, Mantak and Maneewan, and Douglas, Abrams and Rachel. *The Multi Orgasmic Couple: Sexual Secrets Every Couple Should Know,* New York, Harper Collins, 2000

Kerner, Ian. *She Comes First: The Thinking Man's Guide to Pleasuring a Woman,* New York, Harper Collins, 2008

Kingsley, Eve. *Just F**k Me: What Women Want Men to Know About Taking Control in the Bedroom,* Secret Life Publishing, 2011

Lacroix, Nitya. *The Art of Tantric Sex: Ancient Techniques & Rituals That Enhance Sexual Pleasure,* London, Dorling Kindersley Limited, 1997